Unit 1: Biotechnology – An Overview

1.1 What is Biotechnology?

1. Biotechnology is a broad area of biology, involving the use of living systems and organisms to develop or make products. Depending on the tools and applications, it often overlaps with related scientific fields. In the late 20th and early 21st centuries, biotechnology has expanded to include new and diverse sciences, such as genomics, recombinant gene techniques, applied immunology, and development of pharmaceutical therapies and diagnostic tests.

2. The wide concept of "biotech" or "biotechnology" encompasses a wide range of procedures for modifying living organisms according to human purposes, going back to domestication of animals, cultivation of the plants, and "improvements" to these through breeding programs that employ artificial selection and hybridization. Modern usage also includes genetic engineering as well as cell and tissue culture technologies.

3. The American Chemical Society defines biotechnology as the application of biological organisms, systems, or processes by various industries to learning about the science of life and the improvement of the value of materials and organisms such as pharmaceuticals, crops, and livestock. Per the European Federation of Biotechnology, biotechnology is the integration of natural science and organisms, cells, parts thereof, and molecular analogues for products and services.

4. Biotechnology is based on the basic biological sciences (e.g. molecular biology, biochemistry, cell biology, embryology, genetics, microbiology) and conversely provides methods to support and perform basic research in biology.

5. Biotechnology is the research and development in the laboratory using bioinformatics for exploration, extraction, exploitation and production from any living organisms and any source of biomass by means of biochemical engineering where high value-added products could be planned (reproduced by biosynthesis, for example), forecasted, formulated, developed, manufactured, and marketed for the purpose of sustainable operations (for the return from bottomless initial investment on R & D) and gaining durable patents rights (for exclusives rights for sales, and prior to this to receive national and international approval from the results on animal experiment and human experiment, especially on the pharmaceutical branch of biotechnology to prevent any undetected side-effects or safety concerns by using the products).

6. The utilization of biological processes, organisms or systems to produce products that are anticipated to improve human lives is termed biotechnology. By contrast, bioengineering is generally thought of as a related field that more heavily emphasizes higher systems approaches (not necessarily the altering or using of biological materials directly) for interfacing with and utilizing living things. Bioengineering is the application of the principles of engineering and natural sciences to tissues, cells and molecules. This can be considered as the use of knowledge from working with and manipulating biology to achieve a result that can improve functions

in plants and animals. Relatedly, biomedical engineering is an overlapping field that often draws upon and applies biotechnology (by various definitions), especially in certain sub-fields of biomedical or chemical engineering such as tissue engineering, biopharmaceutical engineering, and genetic engineering.

7. Biotechnology is the application of scientific and engineering principles to the processing of materials by biological agents to provide goods and services. From its inception, biotechnology has maintained a close relationship with society. Although now most often associated with the development of drugs, historically biotechnology has been principally associated with food, addressing such issues as malnutrition and famine.

8. The history of biotechnology begins with zymotechnology, which commenced with a focus on brewing techniques for beer. By World War I, however, zymotechnology would expand to tackle larger industrial issues, and the potential of industrial fermentation gave rise to biotechnology. However, both the single-cell protein and gasohol projects failed to progress due to varying issues including public resistance, a changing economic scene, and shifts in political power.

9. Yet the formation of a new field, genetic engineering, would soon bring biotechnology to the forefront of science in society, and the intimate relationship between the scientific community, the public, and the government would ensue. These debates gained exposure in 1975 at the Asilomar Conference, where Joshua Lederberg was the most outspoken supporter for this emerging field in biotechnology.

10. By as early as 1978, with the development of synthetic human insulin, Lederberg's claims would prove valid, and the biotechnology industry grew rapidly. Each new scientific advance became a media event designed to capture public support, and by the 1980s, biotechnology grew into a promising real industry. In 1988, only five proteins from genetically engineered cells had been approved as drugs by the United States Food and Drug Administration (FDA), but this number would skyrocket to over 125 by the end of the 1990s.

1.2 Scope & Importance of Biotechnology

1. Genetic engineering in biotechnology stimulated hopes for both therapeutic proteins, drugs and biological organisms themselves, such as seeds, pesticides, engineered yeasts, and modified human cells for treating genetic diseases. The field of genetic engineering remains a heated topic of discussion in today's society with the advent of gene therapy, stem cell research, cloning, and genetically-modified food.

2. Biotechnology is the applied science and has made advances in two major areas, viz., molecular biology and production of industrially important bio-chemical. The scientists are now diverting themselves toward biotechnological companies; this has caused the development of many biotechnological industries.

3. In USA alone more than 225 companies have been established and successfully working, like Biogen, Cetus, Geneatech, Hybritech, etc. In world, USA, Japan, and many countries of Europe are leaders in biotechnological researchers encouraged by industrialists.

4. These companies are working for human welfare and opted following areas for research and development:

1. Industrial Applications of Biotechnology:

    1. The industrial application of molecular biotechnology is often subdivided, so that we speak of red, green, gray or white biotechnology. This distinction relates to the use of the technology in the medical field (in human and animal medicine), agriculture, the environment and industry.

    2. Some companies also apply knowledge deriving from molecular biotechnology in areas that cut across these distinctions (e.g., in red and green biotechnology, sequencing services). According to an investigation by Ernst and Young relating to the German biotech industry, 92% of companies are currently (2004) working in the field of red biotechnology, 13% in green, and 13% in gray or white biotechnology.

2. Biotechnology in Medicine:

1. Biotechnology-derived pharmaceuticals may be derived from a variety of expression systems such as Escherichia coli, yeast, mammalian, insect or plant cells, transgenic animals or other organisms.

2. The expressed protein or gene may have the identical amino acid or nucleotide sequence as the human endogenous form, or may be intentionally different in sequence to confer some technical advantage such as an optimized pharmacokinetic or pharmacodynamics profile.

3. The glycosylation pattern of protein products is likely to differ from the endogenous human form due to the different glycosylation preferences of the expression system used. Furthermore, intentional post-translation modifications or alterations may be made such as pegylation.

4. It is important for the toxicologist to be aware of the nature of the product to be tested in terms of primary, secondary and tertiary structure, and any post-translational modifications such as glycosylation status, particularly as these may be altered if the manufacturing system is modified.

3. Red Biotechnology:

1. Within the field of red biotechnology, which deals with applications in human and animal medicine, there are various further distinctions that can be made: biopharmaceutical drug development, drug delivery cell and gene therapies, tissue engineering/regenerative medicine, pharmacogenomics (personalized medicine), system biology, and diagnosis using molecular medicine.

4. Green Biotechnology:

1. Green biotechnology is the application of biotechnology processes in agriculture and food production. The main dominant forces in green biotechnology today are agro giants with a worldwide area of operation such as BASF, Bayer Crop-Science, Monsanto and Syngenta.

2. They are concentrating considerable attention on molecular plant biotechnology, which is seen as a future growth factor in agro-industry. The traditional pesticide market, on the other hand has been stagnating for years.

1.3 Branches of Biotechnology

1. Animal Biotechnology: It deals with the development of transgenic animals for increased milk or meat production with resistance to various diseases. It also deals with in vitro fertilization of egg and transfer of embryo to the womb of female animal for further development.

2. Industrial Biotechnology: It deals with commercial production of various useful organic substances, such as acetic acid, citric acid, acetone, glycerine, etc., and antibiotics like penicillin, streptomycin, mitomycin, etc., through the use of microorganisms especially fungi and bacteria.

3. Medical Biotechnology: It deals with diagnosis of various diseases; large scale production of various drugs and hormones such as human insulin and interferon; vaccines for chicken pox, rabies, polio etc. and growth hormones, such as bovine. In the field of medical science, genetic engineering has helped in the large scale production of hormones, blood serum proteins; in the development of antibiotics, and other medically useful products.

4. Environmental Biotechnology: It deals with detoxification of waste and industrial effluents, treatment of sewage water, and control of plant diseases and insects through the use of biological agents, such as viruses, bacteria, fungi etc.

5. Plant Biotechnology: Plant Biotechnology is a combination of tissue culture and genetic engineering. It deals with development of transgenic plants with resistance to biotic and abiotic stress; development of haploids, embryo rescue, clonal multiplication, cryopreservation etc. The main features of plant biotechnology are briefly given below:

1.   Plant biotechnology consists of the application of two basic techniques, viz.,

   1.   Tissue culture
   2.   Recombinant DNA technology

2.   It bypasses sexual process in the development of new crop cultivars.

3.   It makes distant crosses (interspecific and inter-generic) practically feasible.

4.   It helps in the development of transgenic plants (plants with foreign DNA) with resistance to biotic stress.

5.   It is a rapid method of crop improvement. For example, tetraploid plants can be developed in a single step through protoplast fusion.

Unit 2: Animal & Plant Biotechnology

2.1 Plant Tissue Culture

01. Tissue culture is the in vitro aseptic culture of cells, tissues, organs or whole plant under controlled nutritional and environmental conditions often to produce the clones of plants. The resultant clones are true-to type of the selected genotype. The controlled conditions provide the culture an environment conducive for their growth and multiplication. These conditions include proper supply of nutrients, pH medium, adequate temperature and proper gaseous and liquid environment.

02. Plant tissue culture technology is being widely used for large scale plant multiplication. Apart from their use as a tool of research, plant tissue culture techniques have in recent years, become of major industrial importance in the area of plant propagation, disease elimination, plant improvement and production of secondary metabolites.

03. Small pieces of tissue (named explants) can be used to produce hundreds and thousands of plants in a continuous process. A single explant can be multiplied into several thousand plants in relatively short time period and space under controlled conditions, irrespective of the season and weather on a year round basis. Endangered, threatened and rare species have successfully been grown and conserved by micropropagation because of high coefficient of multiplication and small demands on number of initial plants and space.

04.In addition, plant tissue culture is considered to be the most efficient technology for crop improvement by the production of somaclonal and gametoclonal variants. The micropropagation technology has a vast potential to produce plants of superior quality, isolation of useful variants in well-adapted high yielding genotypes with better disease resistance and stress tolerance capacities. Certain type of callus cultures give rise to clones that have inheritable characteristics different from those of parent plants due to the possibility of occurrence of somaclonal variability, which leads to the development of commercially important improved varieties.

05.Commercial production of plants through micropropagation techniques has several advantages over the traditional methods of propagation through seed, cutting, grafting and air-layering etc. It is rapid propagation processes that can lead to the production of plants virus free. Coryodalisyanhusuo, an important medicinal plant was propagated by somatic embryogenesis from tuber-derived callus to produce disease free tubers. Meristem tip culture of banana plants devoid from banana bunchy top virus (BBTV) and brome mosaic virus (BMV) were produced. Higher yields have been obtained by culturing pathogen free germplasmin vitro. Increase in yield up to 150% of virus-free potatoes was obtained in controlled conditions.

06.The science of plant tissue culture takes its roots from the discovery of cell followed by propounding of cell theory. In 1838, Schleiden and Schwann proposed that cell is the basic structural unit of all living organisms. They visualized that cell is capable of autonomy and therefore it should be possible for each cell if given an environment to regenerate into whole plant.

07. Based on this premise, in 1902, a German physiologist, Gottlieb Haberlandt for the first time attempted to culture isolated single palisade cells from leaves in knop's salt solution enriched with sucrose. The cells remained alive for up to one month, increased in size, accumulated starch but failed to divide. Though he was unsuccessful but laid down the foundation of tissue culture technology for which he is regarded as the father of plant tissue culture. After that some of the landmark discoveries took place in tissue culture which are summarized as under:

01.   1902 - Haberlandt proposed concept of in vitro cell culture

02.   1904 - Hannig cultured embryos from several cruciferous species

03.   1922 - Kolte and Robbins successfully cultured root and stem tips respectively

04.   1926 - Went discovered first plant growth hormone –Indole acetic acid

05.   1934 - White introduced vitamin B as growth supplement in tissue culture media for tomato root tip

06.   1939 - Gautheret, White and Nobecourt established endless proliferation of callus cultures

07.   1941 - Overbeek was first to add coconut milk for cell division in Datura

08.   1946 - Ball raised whole plants of *Lupinus* by shoot tip culture

09.   1954 - Muir was first to break callus tissues into single cells

10.   1955 - Skoog and Miller discovered kinetin as cell division hormone

11.   1957 - Skoog and Miller gave concept of hormonal control (auxin: cytokinin) of organ formation

12. 1959 - Reinert and Steward regenerated embryos from callus clumps and cell suspension of carrot (*Daucus carota*)

13. 1960 - Cocking was first to isolate protoplast by enzymatic degradation of cell wall

14. 1960 - Kanta and Maheshwari developed test tube fertilization technique

15. 1960 - Bergmann filtered cell suspension and isolated single cells by plating

16. 1962 - Murashige and Skoog developed MS medium with higher salt concentration

17. 1964 - Guha and Maheshwari produced first haploid plants from pollen grains of Datura (Anther culture)

18. 1966 - Steward demonstrated totipotency by regenerating carrot plants from single cells of tomato

19. 1970 - Power et al. successfully achieved protoplast fusion

20. 1971 - Takebe et al. regenerated first plants from protoplasts

21. 1972 - Carlson produced first interspecific hybrid of *Nicotianatabacum* by protoplast fusion

22. 1974 – Reinhard introduced biotransformation in plant tissue cultures

23. 1977 - Chilton et al. successfully integrated Ti plasmid DNA from Agrobacterium tumefaciens in plants

24. 1978- Melchers et al. carried out somatic hybridization of tomato and potato resulting in pomato

25. 1981- Larkin and Scowcroft introduced the term somaclonal variation

08. In plant cell culture, plant tissues and organs are grown in vitro on artificial media, under aseptic and controlled environment. The technique depends mainly on the concept of totipotentiality of plant cells which refers to the ability of a single cell to express the full genome by cell division. Along with the totipotent potential of plant cell, the capacity of cells to alter their metabolism, growth and development is also equally important and crucial to regenerate the entire plant.

09. Plant tissue culture medium contains all the nutrients required for the normal growth and development of plants. It is mainly composed of macronutrients, micronutrients, vitamins, other organic components, plant growth regulators, carbon source and some gelling agents in case of solid medium. Murashige and Skoog medium (MS medium) is most extensively used for the vegetative propagation of many plant species in vitro. The pH of the media is also important that affects both the growth of plants and activity of plant growth regulators. It is adjusted to the value between 5.4 - 5.8. Both the solid and liquid medium can be used for culturing.

10. The composition of the medium, particularly the plant hormones and the nitrogen source has profound effects on the response of the initial explant. Plant growth regulators (PGR's) play an essential role in determining the development pathway of plant cells and tissues in culture medium. The auxins, cytokinins and gibberellins are most commonly used plant growth regulators. The type and the concentration of hormones used depend mainly on the species of the plant, the tissue or organ cultured and the objective of the experiment.

11. Auxins and cytokinins are most widely used plant growth regulators in plant tissue culture and their amount determined the type of culture established or regenerated. The high concentration of auxins generally favors root formation, whereas the high concentration of cytokinins promotes shoot regeneration. A balance of both auxin and cytokinin leads to the development of mass of undifferentiated cells known as callus.

12. Maximum root induction and proliferation was found in Stevia rebaudiana, when the medium is supplemented with 0.5 mg/l NAA. Cytokinins generally promote cell division and induce shoot formation and axillary shoot proliferation. High cytokinin to auxin ratio promotes shoot proliferation while high auxin to cytokinins ratio results in root formation. Shoot initiation and proliferation was found maximum, when the callus of black pepper was shifted to medium supplemented with BA at the concentration of 0.5 mg/l. Gibberellins are used for enhanced growth and to promote cell elongation. Maximum shoot length was observed in Phalaenopsis orchids when cultured in medium containing 0.5 mg/l GA_3.

2.2 Transgenic Plants

01. Transgenic plants are crops which have been genetically modified with genes from another organism to make the plants more agriculturally productive. Transgenic plants are only those with genes from other species, whereas genetically modified plants can have both new genes and a re-arrangement of the genes already found in the plant. Traditional breeding methods are one form of genetic modification.

02. Transgenic plants have been developed for a variety of reasons: longer shelf life, disease resistance, herbicide resistance, pest resistance, and improved product quality. The first transgenic crop approved for sale in the US, in 1994, was the FlavrSavr tomato, which was intended to have a longer shelf life. There are many controversial issues surrounding the use of transgenic crops. One of the most far-reaching issues is what could happen if these crop plants were to escape from the fields and enter into the environment.

03. Today there are more than 67.7 million hectares (677,000 km²) of transgenic plants being grown throughout the world. There are three general types of transgenic plants; those with genes to improve the quality of the product, those with genes to allow them to resist disease or herbivory (consumption by herbivores, usually insects), and plants with genes that allow them to be resistant to the effects of specific herbicides.

04. Transgenic crops are grown worldwide, although the greatest concentration of transgenic crops is in the United States, at 63% of the world total in 2003. At that time, 81% of the soybeans, 73% of the cotton and 40% of the corn being grown were transgenic. At that time most of the transgenic crops had genes either for herbicide resistance or for insect resistance.

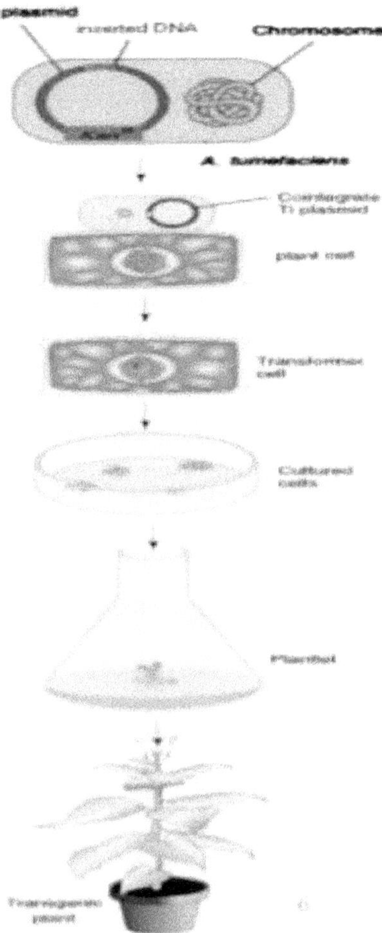

Production of transgenic plants

Isolate and clone gene of interest

Add DNA segments to initiate or enhance gene expression

Add selectable markers

Introduce gene construct into plant cells (transformation)

Select transformed cells or tissues

Regenerate whole plants

2.3 Application of Transgenic Plants

01.Resistance to biotic or abiotic stresses:

1. Biotic stresses occur naturally as a result of stress exerted from other living organism within the same ecosystem. These include bacteria, viruses, herbivores, or native plants. Crop plants are incorporated with disease resistance gene to confer resistance toward these pathogenic diseases that are caused by pest, bacteria, and viruses; this includes tolerance to herbicides.

2. The introduction of genetic modification technology could reduce the usage of expensive pesticides and herbicides in agriculture. The removal of natural pests will lead to a greater yield and better quality of crops. As such, insecticidal toxin genes from a bacterium can be introduced into the plant of interest's genome, thus providing protection to the plant against insect pests. *Bacillus thuringiensis* (Bt) crops are an example of transgenic plant produced through this method. In addition, virus-resistant plants can be achieved through the introduction of viral coat proteins into plants.

3. Development of transgenic plants resistant to abiotic stresses is important in this "Global Warming's Terrifying Era". The world climate in the past few decades has changed tremendously culminating in changes to soil composition, humidity, water, sunlight availability, and many other agricultural problems that led to reduction in the crop yield. Hence, genetic engineering technology is needed as a tool to solve these problems by providing the plants with enhanced stress tolerant ability or protection.

4. The manipulation of transcription factors (TFs), late embryogenesis abundant (LEA) proteins, and antioxidant proteins had successfully produced plants tolerant to drought and salinity. Over–expression of the proline biosynthesis enzyme (P5C), which allows the accumulation of osmoprotectant during drought season provides transgenic plants with osmotic stress resistance.

02. Improving crop yield and nutritional value:

1. Malnutrition is a major health concern that is prevalent especially in the underdeveloped and developing countries due to limited access to nutritious food. Genetic engineering of staple crops has become one of the more effective solutions in addressing this problem. To date, a variety of crops had been successfully modified for better yield as well as for higher nutritional value.

2.   Biofortification is a technique used in agriculture to increase the nutritional value of crops. A well-known example would be the golden rice, a variety of *Oryza sativa*, produced to biosynthesize beta-carotene through genetic modification. The golden rice was developed by adding two beta-carotene synthesis genes: phytoene synthase (psy) and lycopene β-cyclase (β-lcy) (originated from Narcissus pseudonarcissus). These genes were driven under the control of the endosperm-specific glutelin promoter together with a bacterial phytoene desaturase (crtI, from *Erwinia uredovora*).

03. Transgenic plants as bioreactors for recombinant proteins:

1.   Plants had been used as a biofactory in the production of the first recombinant human protein in 1989. Product yields from recombinant proteins using mammalian expression systems are low and expensive, while bacteria system is incapable of post-translational modification in complex protein formation. Due to this, the production methods had shifted to plant cell systems, which provide cheaper and better alternative sources for recombinant proteins production.

2.   The recombinant proteins produced in transgenic plants include antibodies, metabolites or catabolites, proteins, and vaccines. Antibodies and vaccines against gastrointestinal tract diseases, cholera, and malaria are known to be produced in transgenic plants such as potato, banana, algae, and tobacco. An anticancer antibody that recognizes the cells of lung, breast, and colon cancer had also been successfully expressed in rice and wheat seed.

3.   However, despite a lot of successful plant-produced antibodies and vaccines, it is difficult to commercialize them and to date, the only plant-produced Newcastle disease vaccine had been approved by the United States Department of Agriculture for poultry farming with several vaccines in clinical trials.

2.4 Transgenesis

01. Transgenesis is the process of introducing a gene (referred to as a transgene) from one organism into the genome of another organism. The aim is that the resulting transgenic organism will express the gene and exhibit some new property or characteristic. This is made possible by the fact that the genetic code is universal for all living things.

02. Steps involved in the process of transgenesis are outlined below:

1.   Identification:

1.   A gene that codes for a desirable trait or protein must first be identified. Researchers may identify desirable traits in other species and try to identify the gene responsible. There are several techniques that can be used to identify the gene sequence that codes for the specific protein / trait of interest.

2.   If the protein has been isolated it may be possible to determine its amino acid sequence (or part thereof). If the amino acid sequence is know it may be possible to determine part of the gene sequence using a codon table, however there will usually be several different possible sequences due to the redundancy of the genetic code. Once a small part of the sequence has been determined it may be possible to construct a DNA probe that will stick the target gene. Other techniques that may be used to identify a gene include Gene Chips (Microarrays) and DNA Sequencing.

2.   Isolation:

1.   The target gene must then be isolated. DNA from the organism that contains the target gene can usually be isolated simply by breaking up cells mechanically or with chemical treatments such as detergents. The DNA can be separated from the other cell components using a technique call centrifugation. To separate the target gene from the rest of the DNA it would first be cut using a restriction enzyme.

2.   The fragments would then be separated according to size using a technique called Gel Electrophoresis.

3.   The fragment that contains the target gene can be identified using a DNA probe and can then cut out of the gel and amplified (copied) using PCR.

4.   Alternatively the gene could be inserted into a bacterial plasmid using DNA Ligase. The bacteria would then copy the gene each time underwent cell division (a technique called Gene Cloning).

5.   If enough is known about the DNA sequence either side of the gene it may be possible to make specific DNA primers and copy the gene using PCR without first isolating it on a gel.

3.   Transformation:

1.   A vector is then used to transfer the target gene (transgene) into the organism being modified. There are many different vectors / techniques used to transfer the transgene depending on the cell type etc.

2.   However, if the gene is inserted on its own it is unlikely that it will be expressed. Special promotor and termination sequences might be needed either side of the gene in order for it to be expressed. The type of promoter might determine where (in which tissues) the protein is expressed. The final DNA sequence that is prepared including the target gene and associated regulatory sequences is called a Gene Construct.

3.	Most vectors / techniques have low success rates, only producing a very small percentage of cells that actually express the transgene. In order for the gene to be expressed it must make it's way into the nucleus. For it to be passed on during cell division (mitosis and meiosis) it must integrate into the target cells genome (usually by recombination - crossing over). For this reason scientists often incorporate a reporter gene into the gene construct. This is a second gene that codes for an easily selectable / observable characteristic e.g. antibiotic resistance or glow in the dark protein. This makes it easier for researchers to establish while cells have successfully integrated and are expressing the transgene.

2.5 Transgenic Animals

01. Transgenic animals are animals (most commonly mice) that have had a foreign gene deliberately inserted into their genome. Such animals are most commonly created by the microinjection of DNA into the pronuclei of a fertilised egg which is subsequently implanted into the oviduct of a pseudopregnant surrogate mother.

02. Gene manipulation technology is the most important tool considered as the back bone of modern biotechnology. Presently diverse techniques are involved in the production of insulin, growth hormone and monoclonal antibodies. These are the modern medicines produced by the genetically engineered organisms (FDA approved GRAS –generally regarded as safe organisms).

03. Production of human insulin by recombinant *E. coli* is considered as a significant outcome of recombinant DNA technology, more complex proteins of medical uses can also be produced by metabolic and cellular engineering of microorganisms. But production of proteins and other derivatives in its native, functional and intrinsic condition is the ultimate challenge of recombinant technology.

04.Production of Insulin:

1. Insulin is a peptide hormone mainly used in treatment of diabetes mellitus to control elevated blood glucose level. Banting and Best named it originally as 'isletin' and was later renamed as insulin by Macleod, a word that had been suggested in 1910. This hormone is secreted by the βcells of the pancreas and consists of two polypeptide chains, A and B which are linked by two inter-chain and one intra-chain disulphide bridge. Insulin is synthesized as a single-chain precursor, pro-insulin, and produced by the proteolytic processing of pro-insulin in the pancreas.

2. Originally insulin was first identified from dog pancreas which was commercially produced from various sources like foetal calf pancreas obtained from slaughter houses. Now human insulin protein is mass-produced through genetic engineering processes. Recombinant DNA technology has been a great enabler in producing human insulin outside the body for being used as a therapeutic. Insulin is the first human hormone produced in bacteria to be tested in humans for medical purposes.

3.   Recombinant DNA technology has been a great enabler in producing human insulin outside the body for being used as a therapeutic. Insulin is the first human hormone produced in bacteria to be tested in humans for medical purposes. There are many methods for the production of recombinant human insulin in both bacteria and yeast. One typical scheme for preparing human insulin utilizes pro-insulin that is produced in E. coli cytoplasm as an inclusion body of a fusion protein.

4.   Manufacturing of insulin using microbes as a cell factory involves the following steps –

   1.   Isolation of gene: The gene for producing human insulin protein is isolated.

   2.   Preparation of target DNA: Circular piece of DNA called plasmid is obtained from bacteria.

   3.   Insertion of DNA into plasmid: The gene for insulin is inserted into the plasmid construct. The human insulin gene is now recombined with bacterial DNA.

   4.   Plasmid insertion: The bacterial DNA having insulin gene is inserted back into bacteria.

5. Plasmid multiplication: The bacterial cells having insulin gene are allowed to grow and multiply and during this process bacterial cells start to produce recombinant insulin. During division newly synthesized copy of cell are produced.

6. Human insulin produced by bacteria is purified.

Method 1

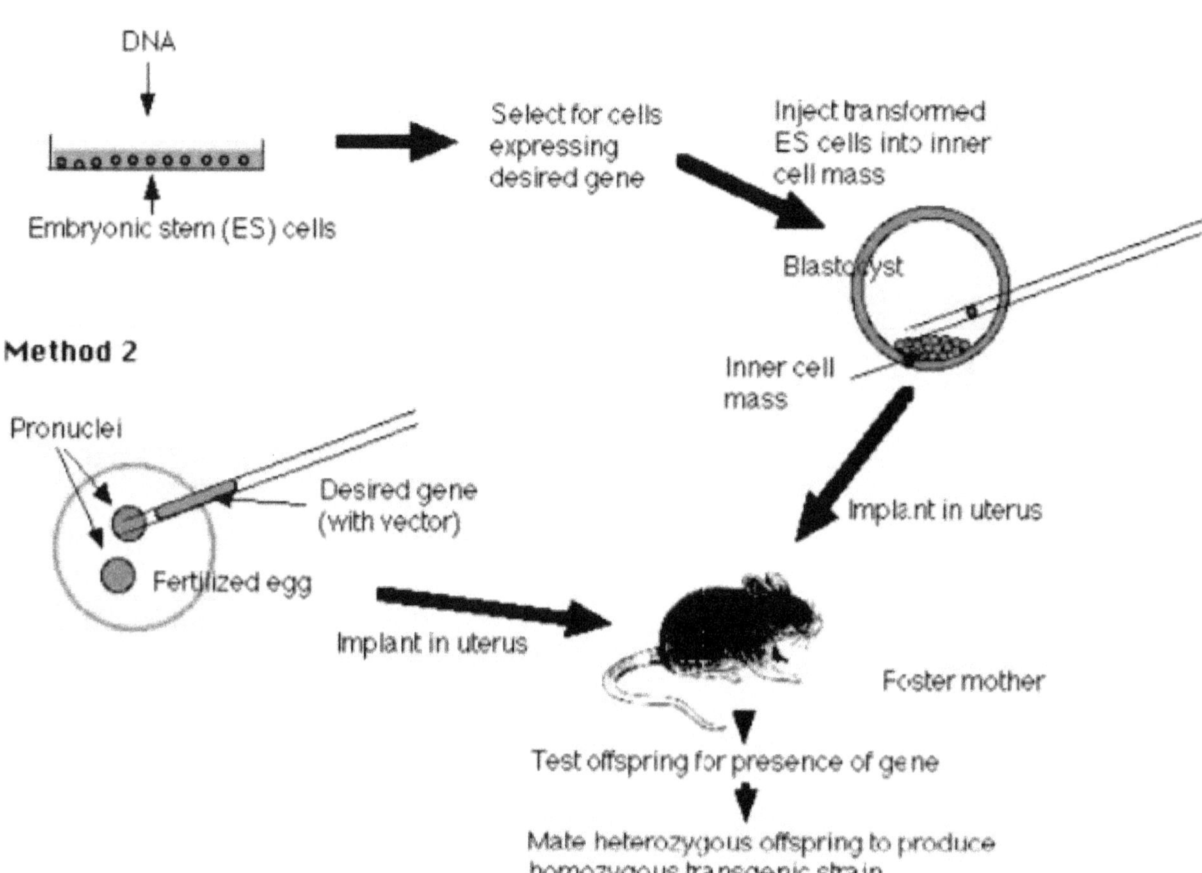

5.   Production of Growth Hormones:

1.   Growth hormone is one of the most important hormones in human body. The core center for production of growth hormone is pituitary gland. The action of growth hormone is either direct or indirect on the human physiological process. But in some children, malfunction of growth hormone results in abnormal growth of the individual. In case of these conditions recombinant growth hormone is useful for the treatment.

2.   Human growth hormone has versatile functions:

   1.   Activates the production of protein in cells by releasing some essential factors.

   2.   Helps in fastening the production of DNA and RNA.

   3.   Accelerates the generation of red blood cells and augments the flow of blood to the kidneys and the rate at which the kidney does its vital filtration work.

   4.   Plays a major role in maintaining the level of fats in the body.

   5.   Activates bone growth and skeletal development indirectly by producing intermediate factor IGF-1.

Hormone	Production host	Engineering approach
Gonadotropin-releasing hormone	*Escherichia coli*	Heterologous expression of the recombinant gonadotropin-releasing hormone in *E. coli* using a T7 RNA polymerase-based expression system and evaluation of various culture conditions on the plasmid stability and the product yield.
Human growth hormone	*Escherichia coli*	Activation of the promoter lambda PL by temperature shift for production of human growth hormone without contaminants.
Human parathyroid hormone	*Escherichia coli*	Using recombinant *E. coli* strain BL21 (DE3) harboring the plasmid. pET32aBI1 encoding the fusion gene of thioredoxin and human parathyroid hormone

Unit 3: Industrial Biotechnology

3.1 Isolation and screening of microorganisms

01. The economics of a fermentation process largely depends upon the type of microorganism used. If fermentation process is to yield a product at a cheaper price the chosen microorganism should give the desired product in a predictable and economically adequate quantity.

02. The microorganism with a desired character is generally isolated from natural substrates like soil etc. Such an organism is generally called as a producer strain.

03. A producer strain should possess the following characters:

   1. It should be able to grow on relatively cheaper substrates.
   2. It should grow well in an ambient temperature preferably at 30-40°C. This reduces the cooling costs.
   3. It should yield high quantity of the end product.
   4. It should possess minimum reaction time with the equipment used in a fermentation process.
   5. It should possess stable biochemical characteristics.
   6. It should yield only the desired substance without producing undesirable substances.
   7. It should possess optimum growth rate so that it can be easily cultivated on a large scale.

04.Detection and isolation of a microorganism from a natural environment like soil containing large number of microbial population is called as screening. It is very time consuming and expensive process. For example, Eli Lilly & Co. Ltd discovered three species of antibiotic producing organisms in a span of 10 years and after screening 4,00,000 organisms.

3.2 Bioreactors

01.Introduction:

1. Bioreactors are closed systems in which a biological process can be carried out under controlled (environmental) conditions.

2. The function of the fermenter or bioreactor is to provide a suitable environment in which an organism can efficiently **produce a target product**—the target product might be:

   1. Cell biomass
   2. Metabolite
   3. Bioconversion Product

3. The sizes of the bioreactor can vary over several orders of magnitudes.

4.   The shake flask (100 -1000 ml), laboratory fermenter (1 – 50 L), pilot scale (0.3 – 10 m^3) to plant scale (2 – 500 m^3) are all examples of bioreactors.

5.   The design and mode of operation of a fermenter mainly depends on:

   1.   the production organism.
   2.   the optimal operating condition required for target product formation.
   3.   product value.
   4.   scale of production.
   5.   the capital investment and running cost.

6.   Large volume and low value products like alcoholic beverages need simple fermenters and do not need aseptic condition.

7.   High value and low volume products require more elaborate system of operation and aseptic condition.

02.Operating Mode of Bioreactor:

1. Batch Reactor:

    1. In this mode, the reactor is filled with medium and the fermentation is allowed to proceed.

    2. When the fermentation has finished the contents are emptied for downstream processing.

    3. The reactor is then cleaned, re-filled, re-inoculated and the fermentation process starts again.

2. Continuous Reactor:

    1. Continuous reactors: fresh media is continuously added and bioreactor fluid is continuously removed.

    2. The reactor can thus be operated for long periods of time without having to be shut down due to the fact that the growth rate of the bacteria in the reactor can be more easily controlled and optimized.

    3. More productive than batch reactors.

4.   Cells can also be immobilized in continuous reactors, to prevent their removal and thus further increase the productivity of these reactors.

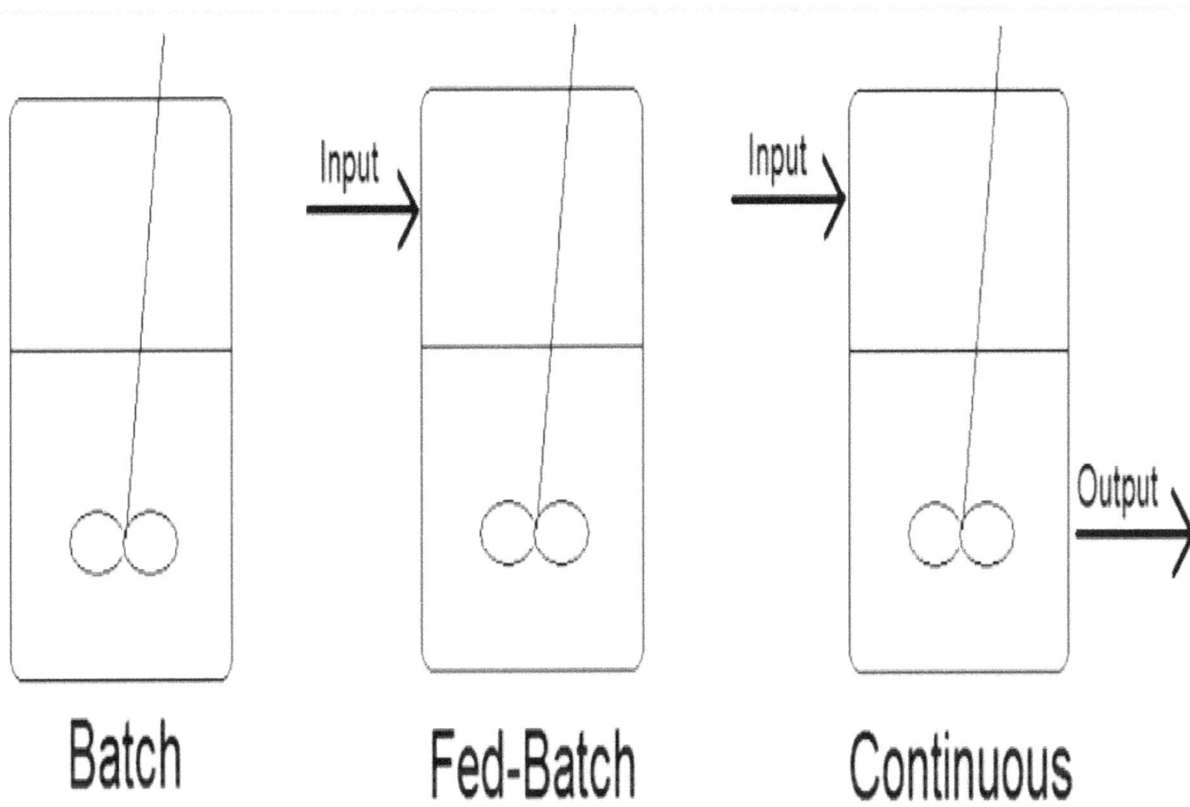

3.   Comparison of Batch Culture and Continuous Cultivation:

Mode of operation	Advantages	Disadvantages
Batch	Versatile: can be used for different reactions every day. Safe: can be properly sterilized. Little risk of infection or strain mutation Complete conversion of substrate is possible	High labor cost: skilled labor is required Much idle time: Sterilization, growth of inoculum, cleaning after the fermentation Safety problems: when filling, emptying, cleaning
Continuous	Works all the time: low labor cost, good utilization of reactor Often efficient: due to the autocatalytic nature of microbial reactions, the productivity can be high. Automation may be very appealing Constant product quality	Often disappointing: promised continuous production for months fails due to a. infection. b. spontaneous mutation of microorganisms to non producing strain Inflexible: can rarely be used for other productions without substantial retrofitting

4.   Types of Cell Culture Bioreactors:

1.   Stirred Tank Bioreactor:

1.   The stirred tank bioreactor is the classical design and still the most widely used bioreactor.

2.   Most production facilities and FDA approved production processes for biopharmaceuticals are based on the stirred tank bioreactors.

3. The scale-up process from laboratory to production sized systems is therefore based on this design as well.

4. This cylindrical bioreactor uses a top or bottom mounted rotating mixing system.

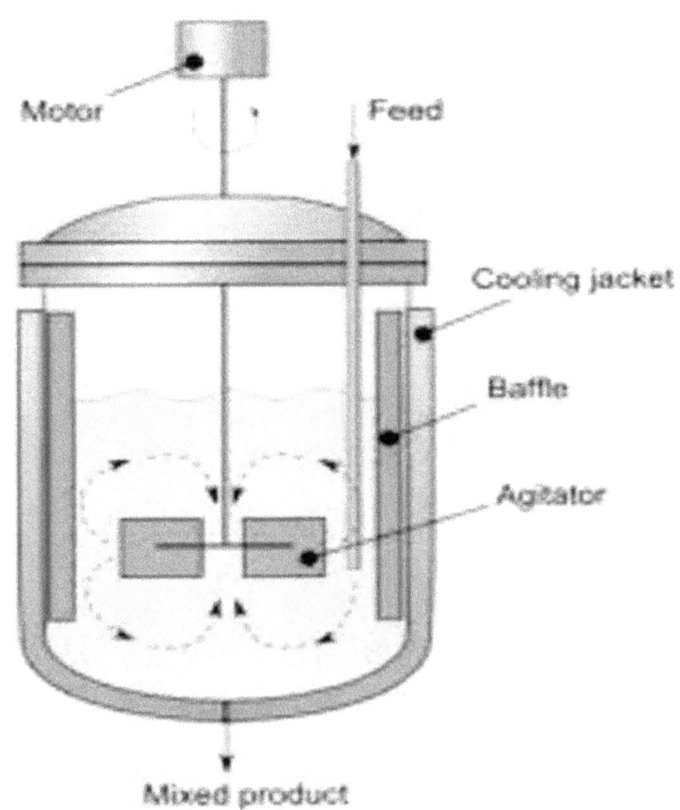

2. Photo bioreactors:

1. A photo bioreactor is a bioreactor that incorporates a light source to provide photonic energy input into the reactor.

2.   Photo bioreactors are used for the cultivation of photosynthesizing organisms (plants, algae, bacteria).

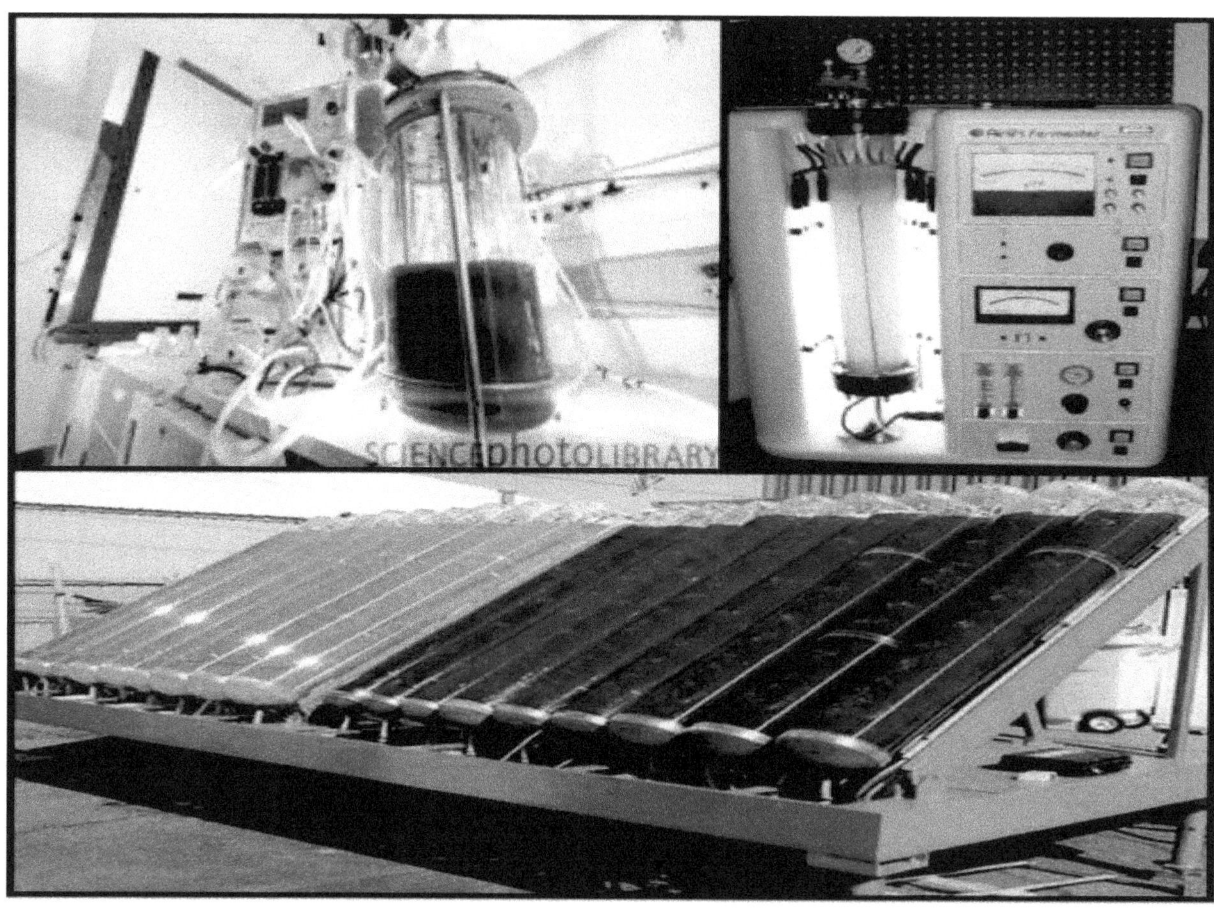

3.   Solid-state bioreactors:

1.   Solid-state bioreactors are used for processes where microorganisms are grown on moist, solid particles.

2.   The spaces between the particles contain a continuous gas phase and a minimum of water.

3.   The majority of SSF processes involve filamentous fungi, although some also involve bacteria or yeasts.

4.   Solid-state fermentation is mainly used in food processes.

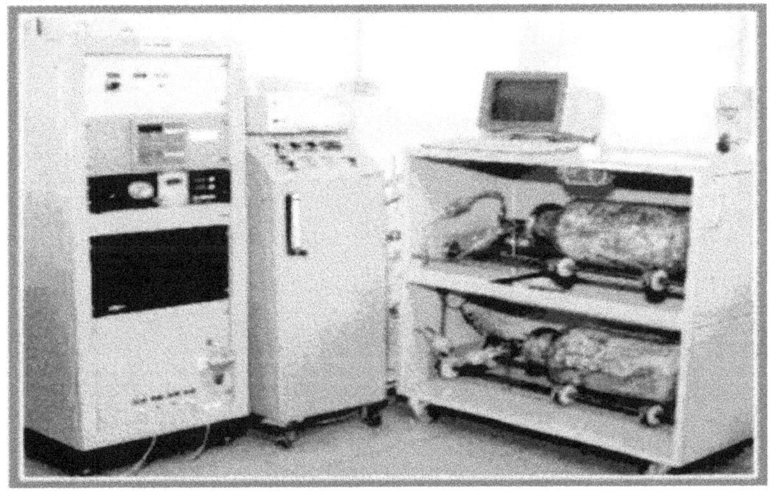

4.	Bubble column bioreactors:

1.	Bubble column bioreactors are tall column bioreactors where gas is introduced in the bottom section for mixing and aeration purposes.

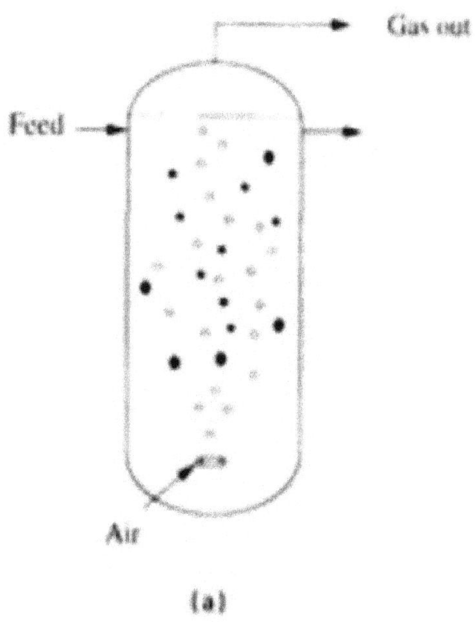

5.   Standard geometry of a stirred tank bioreactor:

1.   A stirred tank reactor will either be approximately cylindrical or have a curved base. A curved base assists in the mixing of the reactor contents.

2.   Stirred tank bioreactors are generally constructed to standard dimensions.

3.   These dimensions take into account both mixing effectiveness and structural considerations.

3.3 Food and Beverage Fermentation

01. It is estimated that about 20-30% of the household budget is spent towards foods in the developed countries. This may be a little less in the developing nations. Therefore, food and beverage biotechnology occupies a prominent place world-over.

02. There are records that man was making bread, wine, curd etc., as early as 4000 BC. These processes, collectively referred to as traditional or old biotechnology, mostly employed for the preparation of foods and beverages, were based on the natural capabilities of the microorganisms (although their existence was unknown at that time).

03. With the advances made in microbiology and recently biotechnology, food and beverage production is a major industry. Food biotechnology is also concerned with the improved quality, nutrition, consistency, colour, safety and preservation of foods, besides making them available round the year (Note: Most foods are seasonal in nature and therefore as such are not available throughout the year). In addition, modern biotechnological processes also take into account the health aspects of the people.

04. The production of fermented foods is variable. This depends on geographical region, availability of raw materials, traditions and food habits of the people. A selected list of fermented foods along with raw materials and fermenting microorganisms is given in Table 28.1.

TABLE 28.1 A selected list of fermented foods along with the raw materials and fermenting organisms

Fermented food/food product (country)	Raw material (substrate)	Fermenting organism(s)
Dairy products		
Cheese (worldwide)	Milk	Streptococcus sp
		Penicillium roquefortii,
		P. camembertii
Yogurt (worldwide)	Milk	Streptococcus thermophilus
		Lactobacillus bulgaricus
Kefir (Russia)	Milk	Lactobacillus sp, Candida sp
Vegetarian products		
Cocoa beans (worldwide)	Cocoa fruit	Candida krusei, Geotrichum sp
Coffee beans (worldwide)	Coffee cherries	Edwinia dissolvens, Saccharomyces sp
Tempeh (Indonesia)	Soy beans	Rhizopus oryzae, Lactobacillus delbrueckiia
Soy sauce (worldwide)	Soy beans	Aspergillus orzyae, A. soyae
Sauekraut (Europe)	Cabbage	Leuconostoc mesenteroides, L. plantarum
Breads (worldwide)	Wheat flour	Saccharomyces cerevisiae
Rolls, cakes (worldwide)	Wheat flour	Saccharomyces cerevisiae
Idli (India)	Rice and black gram	Leuconotoc mesenteroides
Non-vegetarian products		
Dry sausages (worldwide)	Beef, pork	Pedicoccus cerevisiae
Fish sauces (worldwide)	Small fish	Halophilic sp, Bacillus sp
Country-cured hams (worldwide)	Pork, hams	Aspergillus sp, Penicillium sp

05. Advantages of Fermented Foods:

1. Enhanced nutritive value.

2. Increased digestibility.

3. Improved flavour and texture.

4. Serve as supplements in preparing several dishes.

3.4 Production of Antibiotics (ß-lactum antibiotic)

01. An antibiotic is a type of antimicrobial substance active against bacteria. It is the most important type of antibacterial agent for fighting bacterial infections, and antibiotic medications are widely used in the treatment and prevention of such infections. They may either kill or inhibit the growth of bacteria. A limited number of antibiotics also possess antiprotozoal activity. Antibiotics are not effective against viruses such as the common cold or influenza; drugs which inhibit viruses are termed antiviral drugs or antivirals rather than antibiotics.

02. Sometimes, the term antibiotic—literally "opposing life", from the Greek roots ἀντι anti, "against" and βίος bios, "life"—is broadly used to refer to any substance used against microbes, but in the usual medical usage, antibiotics (such as penicillin) are those produced naturally (by one microorganism fighting another), whereas nonantibiotic antibacterials (such as sulfonamides and antiseptics) are fully synthetic.

03. However, both classes have the same goal of killing or preventing the growth of microorganisms, and both are included in antimicrobial chemotherapy. "Antibacterials" include antiseptic drugs, antibacterial soaps, and chemical disinfectants, whereas antibiotics are an important class of antibacterials used more specifically in medicine and sometimes in livestock feed.

04. Antibiotics have been used since ancient times. Many civilizations used topical application of mouldy bread, with many references to its beneficial effects arising from ancient Egypt, Nubia, China, Serbia, Greece, and Rome. The first person to directly document the use of moulds to treat infections was John Parkinson (1567–1650). Antibiotics revolutionized medicine in the 20th century.

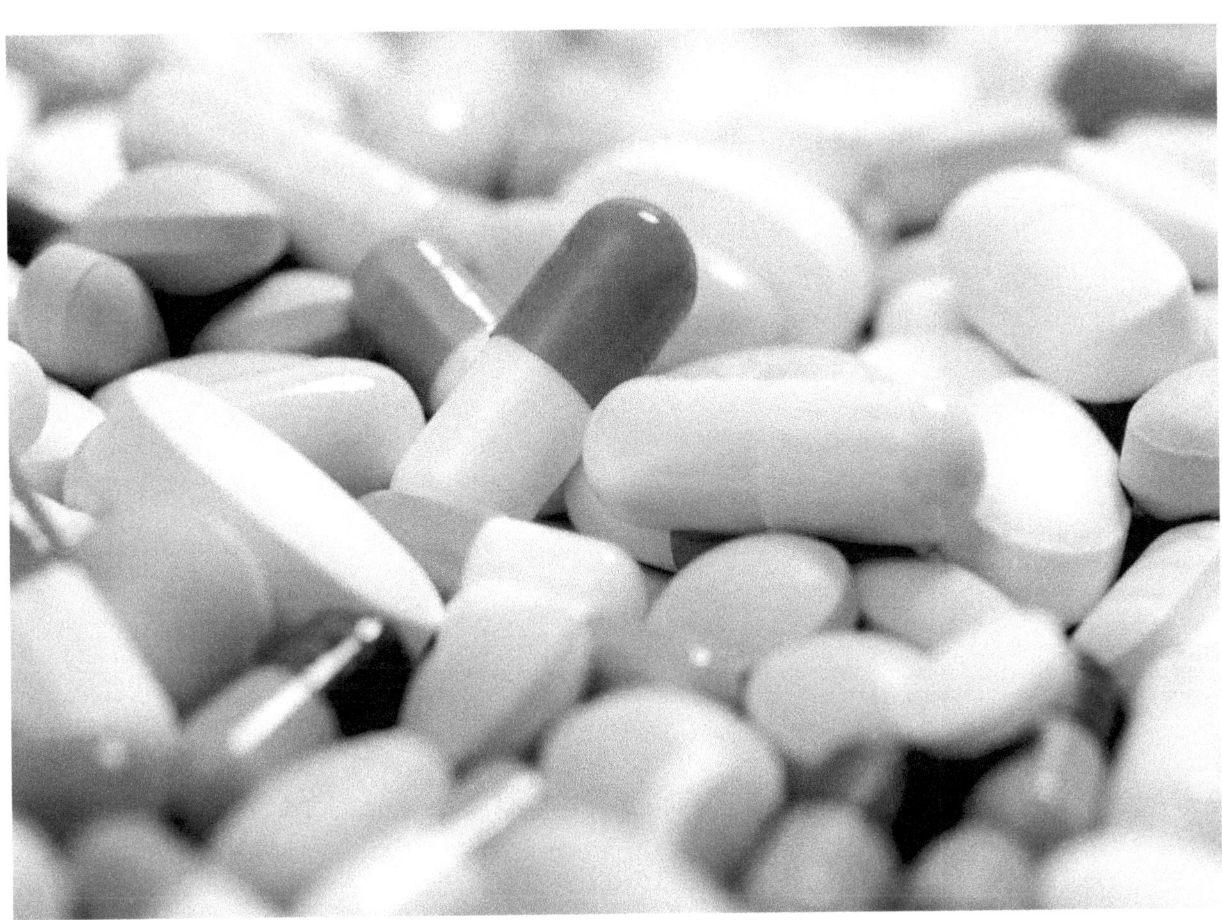

05.Penicillin:

1. Penicillin G (benzylpenicillin) was the first β-lactam to be used clinically, most frequently to treat streptococcal infections for which it had high potency (Rammelkamp and Keefer 1943; Hirsh and Dowling 1946). Another naturally occurring penicillin, penicillin V (phenoxymethylpenicillin), in an oral formulation is still used therapeutically and prophylactically for mild to moderate infections caused by susceptible Streptococcus spp., including use in pediatric patients (Pottegard et al. 2015).

2. However, the selection of penicillin-resistant penicillinase-producing staphylococci in patients treated with penicillin G led to decreased use of this agent, and prompted the search for more penicillins with greater stability to the staphylococcal β-lactamases (Kirby 1944, 1945; Medeiros 1984).

3. A list of historically important and clinically useful penicillins is provided in Table 2. Among the penicillinase-stable penicillins of clinical significance are methicillin, oxacillin, cloxacillin, and nafcillin, with the latter suggested as the β-lactam of choice for skin infections, catheter infections, and bacteremia caused by methicillin-susceptible S. aureus (Bamberger and Boyd 2005). All were used primarily for staphylococcal infections until the emergence of methicillin-resistant S. aureus (MRSA) in 1979–1980 (Hemmer et al. 1979; Saroglou et al. 1980).

Table 2. Penicillins of current and historical utility

Name	R_1	R_2	Route of administration	Approval date[b,c]	Status
Benzylpenicillin (penicillin G)	—H		IM or IV	1946	Approved worldwide
Phenoxymethylpenicillin (penicillin V)	—H		Oral	1968	Approved worldwide
Methicillin	—H		IV	1960	No longer available; of historical interest
Oxacillin	—H		Oral, IV	1962	Widely available, but not in the United Kingdom
Cloxacillin	—H		Oral, IV	1974	Widely available, but not in the United Kingdom
Ampicillin	—H		Oral, IV	1963	Widely available
Nafcillin	—H		IV	1970	Limited availability
Amoxicillin	—H		Oral, IV	1972	Widely available
Carbenicillin	—H		Oral	1972	Discontinued
Ticarcillin	—H		IV	1976	Limited availability
Piperacillin	—H		IV	1981	Widely available, primarily in combination with tazobactam
Temocillin	—OCH₃		IV	1985 in Europe (Harvengt 1985)	Limited availability (Europe)
Mecillinam			IV	1978	Limited availability

IM, Intramuscular; IV, intravenous.
[a]FDA approval unless otherwise noted.
[b]Dates were updated from Medeiros (1997) (www.accessdata.fda.gov/scripts/cder/drugsatfda; www.drugs.com).

4.   Penicillins with improved activity against Gram-negative pathogens included the orally bioavailable ampicillin and amoxicillin, both of which were introduced in the 1970s. These agents were initially used for the treatment of infections caused by *Enterobacteriaceae* and did not effectively inhibit the growth of *Pseudomonas aeruginosa*, which became more of a concern during the late 1970s.

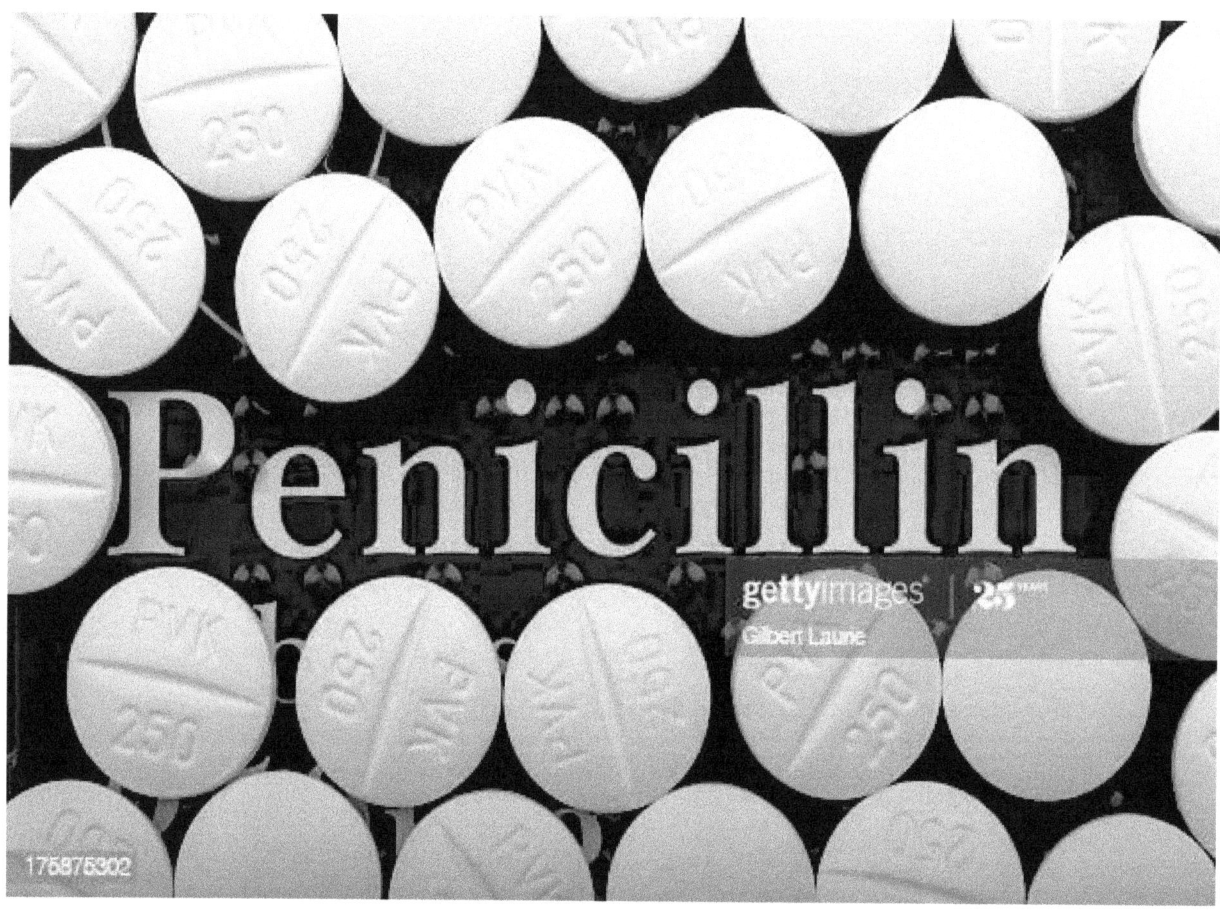

06.Cephalosporin:

1. During the 1950s, the discovery of the naturally occurring penicillinase-stable cephalosporin C opened a new pathway to the development of hundreds of novel cephalosporins (Newton and Abraham 1956; Abraham 1987) to treat infections caused by the major penicillinase-producing pathogen of medical interest at that time, S. aureus. Dozens of cephalosporins were introduced into clinical practice (Abraham 1987), either as parenteral or oral agents.

2. The molecules exhibited antibacterial activity with MICs often $\leq$4 µg/mL against not only staphylococci, but also Streptococcus pneumoniae and non-β-lactamase-producing enteric bacteria. The parenteral agents were generally eightfold more potent than the oral agents that were used in some cases to replace oral penicillins in penicillin-allergic patients.

3. The early cephalosporins, for example, those in the cephalosporin I subclass (Bryskier et al. 1994) introduced before 1980, were labile to hydrolysis by many β-lactamases that emerged following their introduction into clinical practice, so that only a few of the early molecules remain in use (see Table 3), primarily to treat mild to moderate skin infections caused by methicillin-susceptible S. aureus (MSSA) (Giordano et al. 2006).

4. Cefazolin with high biliary concentrations is still used for surgical prophylaxis and for treatment of abdominal infections (Sudo et al. 2014) and is effective as empiric therapy in 80% of Japanese children with their first upper urinary tract infection (Abe et al. 2016).

Table 3. Cephalosporins of current clinical utility or of historical interest

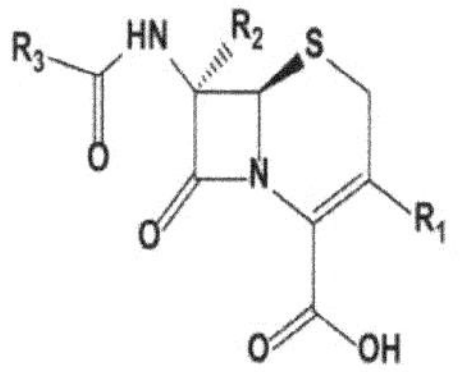

Name	Subclass[a]	R_1	R_2	R_3	Route of administration	Approval date[b,c]	Status
Cephalexin	Cephalosporin I	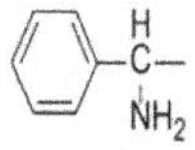 (phenyl–CH(NH$_2$)–)	–H	–CH$_3$	Oral	1971	Limited availability
Cefaclor	Cephalosporin I	–Cl	–H	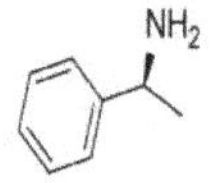 (phenyl–CH(NH$_2$)–CH$_3$)	Oral	1979	Widely available
Cefixime	Cephalosporin V	 (vinyl)	–H	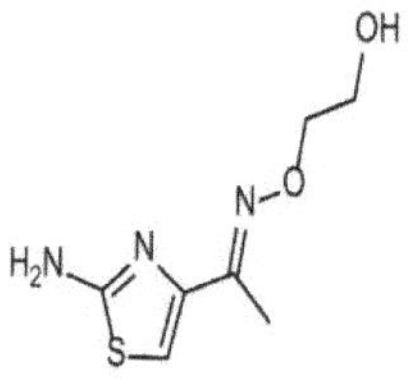 (aminothiazole–C(=N–O–CH$_2$CH$_2$OH)–)	Oral	1989	Widely available
Cefpodoxime	Cephalosporin IV	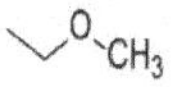 (–CH$_2$–O–CH$_3$)	–H	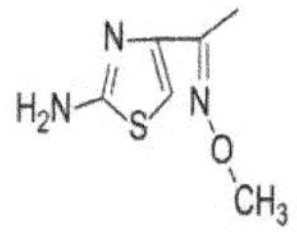 (aminothiazole–C(=N–O–CH$_3$)–)	Oral	1992	Widely available
Ceftibutin	Cephalosporin III	–H	–H	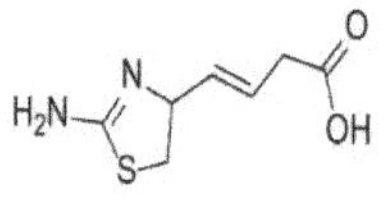 (aminothiazole–CH–CH=CH–COOH)	Oral	1995	Widely available

5.   When the TEM-1 penicillinase began to appear on transmissible plasmids in Neisseria gonorrhoeae (Ashford et al. 1976) and Haemophilus influenzae (Gunn et al. 1974; Khan et al. 1974), it was quickly recognized that the penicillins and cephalosporins in medical use were becoming ineffective, not only in treating those TEM-1-producing organisms, but also for the enteric bacteria and P. aeruginosa that could all acquire this enzyme. Another surge of synthetic activity in the pharmaceutical industry provided both oral and parenteral cephalosporins with stability to this common enzyme.

6.   These agents tended to have decreased potency against the staphylococci, but gained antibacterial activity against Gram-negative pathogens. Cefuroxime, dosed parenterally or orally as the axetil ester, was the only member of the cephalosporin II class (Bryskier et al. 1994) with both oral and systemic dosage forms, but its stability to β-lactamase hydrolysis was diminished compared to later oral cephalosporins (Jacoby and Carreras 1990).

7.   As seen with cefuroxime, acceptable oral bioavailability of cefpodoxime required esterification through addition of a proxetil group to attain sufficient absorption for efficacy (Bryskier and Belfiglio 1999). Of the oral agents approved after 1983 in Table 3, cefdinir was generally more stable to hydrolysis, not only to the original TEM enzyme, but also to the AmpC cephalosporinases that are produced at a basal level in many enteric bacteria and P. aeruginosa (Payne and Amyes 1993; Labia and Morand 1994).

8. Among the parenteral agents introduced in the 1980s were the cephamycin cefoxitin, and cephalosporins in the cephalosporin III and cephalosporin IV subclasses (Bryskier et al. 1994), which continue to serve as important antibiotics for the treatment of serious infections caused by Gram-negative pathogens.

3.5 Enzymes

01.Amylase

1. An amylase is an enzyme that catalyses the hydrolysis of starch (Latin amylum) into sugars. Amylase is present in the saliva of humans and some other mammals, where it begins the chemical process of digestion. Foods that contain large amounts of starch but little sugar, such as rice and potatoes, may acquire a slightly sweet taste as they are chewed because amylase degrades some of their starch into sugar.

2. The pancreas and salivary gland make amylase (alpha amylase) to hydrolyse dietary starch into disaccharides and trisaccharides which are converted by other enzymes to glucose to supply the body with energy. Plants and some bacteria also produce amylase. Specific amylase proteins are designated by different Greek letters. All amylases are glycoside hydrolases and act on α-1,4-glycosidic bonds.

	α-amylase	β-amylase	γ-amylase
Source	Animals, plants, microbes	Plants, microbes	Animals, microbes
Tissue	Saliva, pancreas	Seeds, fruits	Small intestine
Cleavage site	Random α-1,4 glycosidic bond	Second α-1,4 glycosidic bond	Last α-1,4 glycosidic bond
Reaction products	Maltose, dextrin, etc	Maltose	Glucose
Optimum pH	6.7–7.0	4.0–5.0	3.0
Optimum temperature in brewing	63–70 °C	55–65 °C	

02.Protease:

1. A protease (also called a peptidase or proteinase) is a Trypsin that catalyzes (increases the rate of) proteolysis, the breakdown of proteins into smaller polypeptides or single amino acids. They do this by cleaving the peptide bonds within proteins by hydrolysis, a reaction where water breaks bonds. Proteases are involved in many biological functions, including digestion of ingested proteins, protein catabolism (breakdown of old proteins), and cell signalling.

2. Without additional helping mechanisms, proteolysis would be very slow, taking hundreds of years. Proteases can be found in all forms of life and viruses. They have independently evolved multiple times, and different classes of protease can perform the same reaction by completely different catalytic mechanisms.

3.5 Biotransformation

01.Biotransformation is the chemical modification (or modifications) made by an organism on a chemical compound. If this modification ends in mineral compounds like CO_2, NH_4^+, or H_2O, the biotransformation is called mineralisation.

02. Biotransformation means chemical alteration of chemicals such as nutrients, amino acids, toxins, and drugs in the body. It is also needed to render non-polar compounds polar so that they are not reabsorbed in renal tubules and are excreted. Biotransformation of xenobiotics can dominate toxicokinetics and the metabolites may reach higher concentrations in organisms than their parent compounds. Recently its application is seen as an efficient, cost effective, and easily applicable approach for the valorization of agricultural wastes with potentials of enhancing existing bioactive components and synthesis of new compounds.

03. Drug metabolism:

1. The metabolism of a drug or toxin in a body is an example of a biotransformation. The body typically deals with a foreign compound by making it more water-soluble, to increase the rate of its excretion through the urine. There are many different processes that can occur; the pathways of drug metabolism can be divided into:

   1. Phase I reaction:

      1. Includes oxidative, reductive, and hydrolytic reactions.

      2. In these types of reactions, a polar group is either introduced or unmasked, so the drug molecule becomes more water-soluble and can be excreted.

3.   Reactions are non-synthetic in nature and in general produce a more water-soluble and less active metabolites.

4.   The majority of metabolites are generated by a common hydroxylating enzyme system known as Cytochrome P450.

2.   Phase II reaction:

1.   These reactions involve covalent attachment of small hydrophilic endogenous molecule such as glucuronic acid, sulfate, or glycine to form water-soluble compounds, that are more hydrophilic.

2.   This is also known as a conjugation reaction.

3.   The final compounds have a larger molecular weight.

04.Microbial biotransformation:

1. Biotransformation of various pollutants is a sustainable way to clean up contaminated environments. These bioremediation and biotransformation methods harness the naturally occurring, microbial catabolic diversity to degrade, transform or accumulate a huge range of compounds including hydrocarbons (e.g. oil), polychlorinated biphenyls (PCBs), polyaromatic hydrocarbons (PAHs), pharmaceutical substances, radionuclides and metals. Major methodological breakthroughs in recent years have enabled detailed genomic, metagenomic, proteomic, bioinformatic and other high-throughput analyses of environmentally relevant microorganisms providing unprecedented insights into biotransformation and biodegradative pathways and the ability of organisms to adapt to changing environmental conditions.

2. Biological processes play a major role in the removal of contaminants and pollutants from the environment. Some microorganisms possess an astonishing catabolic versatility to degrade or transform such compounds. New methodological breakthroughs in sequencing, genomics, proteomics, bioinformatics and imaging are producing vast amounts of information. In the field of Environmental Microbiology, genome-based global studies open a new era providing unprecedented in silico views of metabolic and regulatory networks, as well as clues to the evolution of biochemical pathways relevant to biotransformation and to the molecular adaptation strategies to changing environmental conditions.

Unit 4: Medical Biotechnology

4.1 Conventional Vaccines

01.Classification:

1. Conventional vaccines originate from viruses or bacteria and can be divided in live attenuated vaccines and non-living vaccines. In addition, three vaccine generations can be distinguished for non-living vaccines.

    1. 1st generation vaccines consist of an inactivated suspension of the pathogenic microorganism. Little or no purification is applied.

    2. For 2nd generation vaccines purification steps are applied, varying from the purification of a pathogenic micro-organism (e.g., improved non-living polio vaccine) to the complete purification of the protective component (e.g., polysaccharide vaccines).

    3. 3rd generation vaccine are either a well-defined combination of protective components (e.g., acellular pertussis vaccine) or the protective component with the desired immunological properties (e.g., polysaccharides conjugated with carrier proteins).

2. An overview of the various groups of conventional vaccines and their generations is given in Table

Type	Example	Marketed	Characteristics[a]
Live			
Viral	Adenovirus	Yes	Oral vaccine, USA military services only, whole
	Poliovirus (Sabin)	Yes	Whole
	Hepatitis A virus	No	
	Measles virus	Yes	
	Mumps virus	Yes	
	Rubella virus	Yes	
	Varicella zoster virus	Yes	
	Vaccinia virus	Yes	
	Yellow fever virus	Yes	
	Rotavirus	No	
	Influenza virus	No	
Bacterial	Bacille Calmette–Guérin	Yes	Inactivated whole organism, oral vaccine
	Salmonella typhi	Yes	Inactivated whole
Non-living (first generation products)			
Viral	Poliovirus (Salk)	Yes	Purified inactivated whole
	Influenza virus	Yes	
	Japanese B encephalitis virus	Yes	

		Live[a]	
Bacterial	Bordetella pertussis	Yes	
	Vibrio cholerae	Yes	
	Salmonella typhi	Yes	
Non-living (second generation products)			
Viral	Poliovirus	Yes	
	Rabies virus	Yes	
	Hepatitis A virus	Yes	
	Influenza virus	Yes	Subunit vaccine
	Hepatitis B virus	Yes	Plasma-derived hepatitis B surface antigen
Bacterial	Bordetella pertussis	Yes	Bacterial protein extract
	Haemophilus influenzae type b	Yes	Capsular polysaccharides
	Neisseria meningitidis	Yes	Capsular polysaccharides
	Streptococcus pneumoniae	Yes	Capsular polysaccharides
	Vibrio cholerae	Yes	Bacterial suspension + B subunit of cholera toxin
	Corynebacterium diphtheriae	Yes	Diphtheria toxoid
	Clostridium tetani	Yes	Tetanus toxoid
Non-living (third generation products)			
Viral	Measles virus	No	Subunit vaccine, ISCOM formulation
Bacterial	Bordetella pertussis	Yes	Mixture of purified protein antigens
	Haemophilus influenzae type B	Yes	Polysaccharide-protein conjugates
	Neisseria meningitidis	No	Polysaccharide-protein conjugates
	Streptococcus pneumoniae	No	Polysaccharide-protein conjugates

[a] Unless mentioned otherwise, the vaccine is administered parenterally.
Source: From Plotkin and Orenstein, 2004.

Table 4 Conventional vaccines.

02.Live Attenuated Vaccines:

1. Before the introduction of recombinant-DNA (rDNA) technology, a first step to improved live vaccines was the attenuation of virulent microorganisms by serial passage and selection of mutant strains with reduced virulence or toxicity. Examples are vaccine strains for oral polio vaccine, measles-rubella-mumps (MMR) combination vaccine, and tuberculosis vaccine consisting of bacille Calmette-Gue´rin (BCG). An alternative approach is chemical mutagenesis. For instance, by treating *Salmonella typhi* with nitrosoguanidine, a mutant strain lacking some enzymes that are responsible for the virulence was isolated (Germanier and Fuer, 1975).

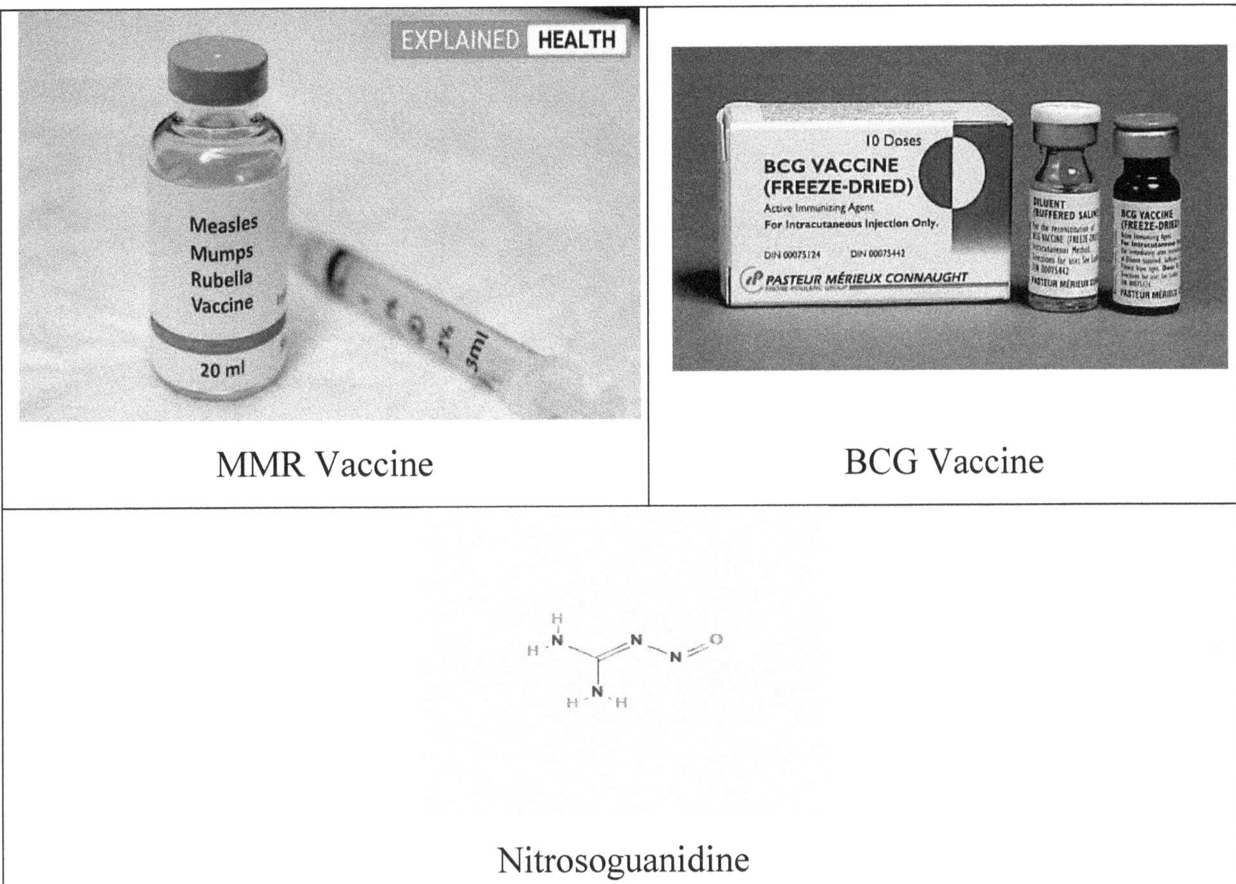

MMR Vaccine

BCG Vaccine

Nitrosoguanidine

2. Live attenuated organisms have a number of advantages as vaccines over non-living vaccines. After administration, live vaccines may replicate in the host similar to their pathogenic counterparts. This confronts the host with a larger and more sustained dose of antigen, which means that few and low doses are required. In general, the vaccines give long-lasting humoral and cell-mediated immunity.

3.	Live vaccines also have drawbacks. Live viral vaccines bear the risk that the nucleic acid is incorporated into the host's genome. Moreover, reversion to a virulent form may occur, although this is unlikely when the attenuated seed strain contains several mutations. Nevertheless, for diseases such as viral hepatitis, AIDS and cancer, this drawback makes the use of conventional live vaccines virtually unthinkable.

4.	Furthermore, it is important to recognize that immunization of immunodeficient children with live organisms can lead to serious complications. For instance, a child with T-cell deficiency may become overwhelmed with BCG and die.

4.2 Recombinant Vaccines

01. Several genes from different etiologic agents have been cloned, expressed and purified to be tested as vaccines. There are a variety of expression systems for antigenic protein components, such as bacteria, yeast, mammalian cells and insect cells, in which the DNA encoding the antigenic determinant can be inserted and expressed. However, several factors must be taken into account before selecting the system for antigen expression.

02. The level of expression obtained using each specific expression vector and promoter, the selection marker of choice, the presence or absence of post-translational modification by the recombinant vector, among others, are essential features that interfere in the efficacy of production of recombinant antigens as vaccines. Bacterial expression systems are the most used due to the ease of handling and to their capacity for high level expression. However, for antigens in which post-translational modifications (e.g., glycosylation) are necessary, the use of mammalian or insect cells should be considered.

03. Recombinant protein vaccines:

   1. Most of the vaccines under investigation today are based on highly purified recombinant proteins or subunits of pathogens. The classical example of recombinant protein vaccines currently in use in humans is the vaccine against hepatitis B (Table 1). Hepatitis B virus (HBV) infection is a chronic liver disease occurring worldwide.

2.   HBV presents a marked tropism for human liver cells, partially due to a specific receptor that is expressed on the surface of infected cells. The current vaccines are produced by expressing the hepatitis B surface antigen (HBsAg) in yeast cells. The HBsAg assembles into virus-like particles (VLPs), which are extremely immunogenic, making the HBV vaccine a very efficacious vaccine. The yeast expression system may secrete the antigen into the culture supernatant that can facilitate its purification.

3.   Furthermore, yeast cells offer some of the eukaryotic cellular machinery responsible for the post-translational modification of proteins, being capable of rendering proteins glycosylated. The technology of production of the HBV vaccine has been transferred to several manufacturers and the prices have decreased due to competition, which has rendered this vaccine affordable to most developing countries.

Table 1.
Licensed[a] viral and bacterial vaccines for use in humans.

	Live attenuated	Killed inactivated	Subunit
Viral	Vaccinia	Polio (IPV)	Hepatitis B (HepB-surface antigen)
	Polio (OPV)	Rabies	Human papilloma virus (HPV)
	Yellow fever	Influenza	
	Measles	Hepatitis A	
	Mumps		
	Rubella		
	Influenza		
	Rotavirus		
Bacterial	BCG (tuberculosis)	*Bordetella pertussis* (whole cell)	Tetanus (toxoid)
	Salmonella typhi (oral)	Cholera	Diphtheria (toxoid)
		Bacillus anthracis	*Neisseria meningitidis* (polysaccharide)
			Bordetella pertussis (acellular)
			Streptococcus pneumoniae, 23 valent (polysaccharide)
			Haemophilus influenzae, type b (Hib) (polysaccharide)
			Neisseria meningitidis (polysaccharide conjugate)
			Streptococcus pneumoniae, heptavalent (conjugate polysaccharides)
			Salmonella typhi Vi (capsular polysaccharide)

[a]Licensed by national regulatory agencies such as ANVISA in Brazil or FDA in the USA.
OPV = oral polio vaccine; IPV = inactivated polio vaccine; BCG = bacillus Calmette-Guérin.

04.Live recombinant vaccines using bacterial or viral vectors:

1.   As a result of advances in the fields of molecular biology and genetic engineering it is now possible to create live recombinant vectors capable of delivering heterologous antigens by the introduction of antigen-encoding genes. The idea behind this approach is to use the capacity of infection and the immunological properties of the live vector to elicit an immune response against its own proteins, as well as towards the heterologous protein being presented.

2.   A number of bacteria [such as *Salmonella typhi* and bacille Calmette-Guérin (BCG)] and viruses [such as vaccinia (smallpox) and adenovirus] have been investigated as live recombinant vector vaccines. In general, these approaches have advantages that are intrinsic to the pathogen itself, such as mimicry of a natural infection, their capacity of stimulating both $CD4^+$ and $CD8^+$ T-cell subsets, and, in some cases, the possibility to be administered orally.

3.   The use of live-attenuated bacterial vaccines is not novel. However, their utilization as carriers or delivery vehicles for heterologous antigen expression represents a technology with broad applicability that may have a significant impact on vaccine development. Significant advances in molecular biology have enabled precise deletions of genes encoding important virulence factors, as well as the introduction of recombinant DNA into avirulent yet immunogenic vaccine strains.

4.	Bacterial vectors have many advantages that make them attractive systems for heterologous antigen presentation. They can elicit humoral and/or cellular immune responses and can be administered orally, thereby eliciting mucosal immunity. Most are antibiotic-sensitive strains, which allow antibiotic treatment if any adverse reaction occurs. In general, they display very favorable cost-effectiveness.

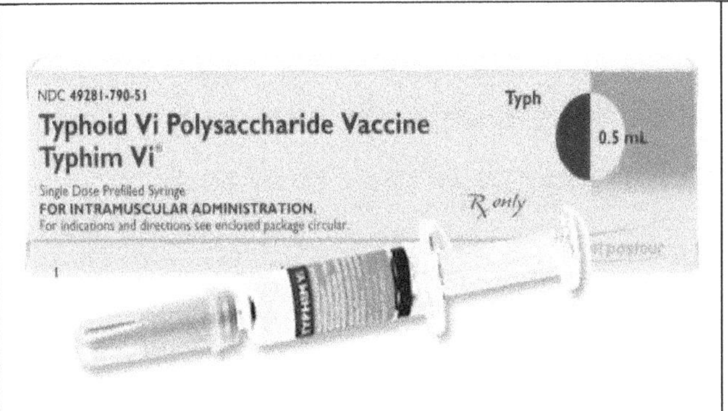

Mycobacterium bovis BCG vaccine

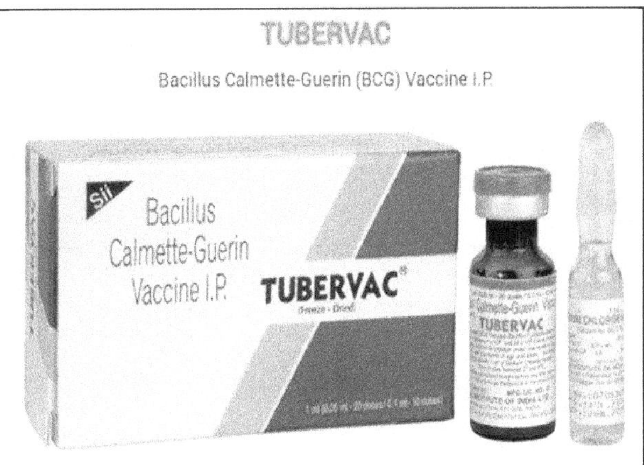

BCG Vaccine

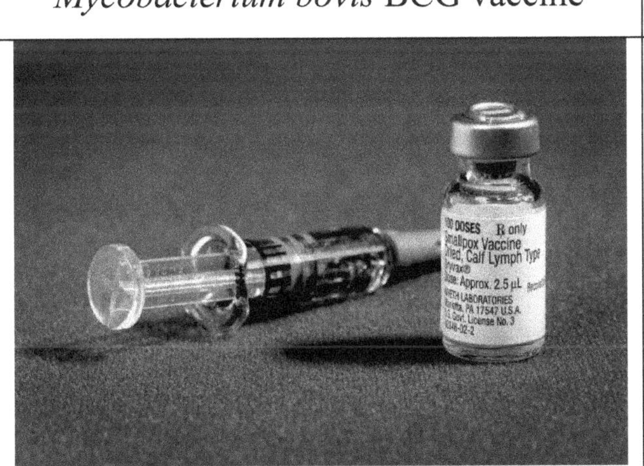

Vaccinia (Smallpox) vaccine

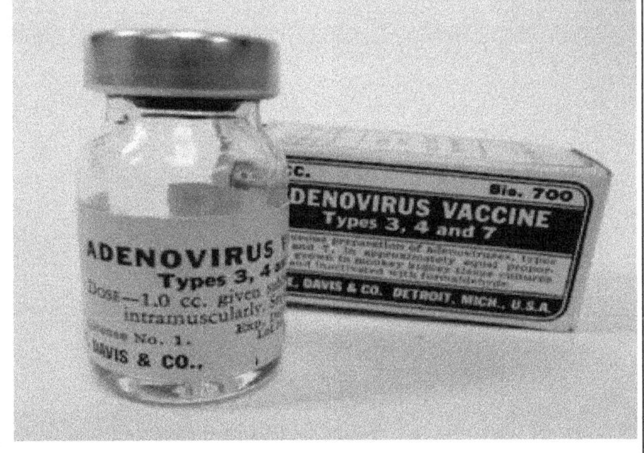

Adenovirus vaccine

4.3 DNA Vaccines

01. DNA vaccination is a technique for protecting an organism against disease by injecting it with genetically engineered DNA to produce an immunological response. Nucleic acid vaccines are still experimental, and have been applied to a number of viral, bacterial and parasitic models of disease, as well as to several tumour models. DNA vaccines have a number of advantages over conventional vaccines, including the ability to induce a wider range of immune response types.

02. Vaccines are among the greatest achievements of modern medicine – in industrial nations, they have eliminated naturally-occurring cases of smallpox, and nearly eliminated polio, while other diseases, such as typhus, rotavirus, hepatitis A and B and others are well controlled. Conventional vaccines, however, only cover a small number of diseases, and infections that lack effective vaccines kill millions of people every year, with AIDS, hepatitis C and malaria being particularly common.

03. The vaccine DNA is injected into the cells of the body, where the "inner machinery" of the host cells "reads" the DNA and converts it into pathogenic proteins. Because these proteins are recognised as foreign, they are processed by the host cells and displayed on their surface, to alert the immune system, which then triggers a range of immune responses. These DNA vaccines developed from "failed" gene therapy experiments.

04.A DNA vaccine (or genetic vaccine as it is also called) consists of a plasmid containing:

1. One origin of replication of *Escherichia coli*, for the amplification of the plasmid
2. A strong promoter, generally from cytomegalovirus
3. Multiple Cloning Sites, in which one can insert the gene to be expressed
4. An antibiotic as selection marker

05.The first demonstration of a plasmid-induced immune response was when mice inoculated with a plasmid expressing human growth hormone elicited antibodies instead of altering growth. Thus far, few experimental trials have evoked a response sufficiently strong enough to protect against disease, and the usefulness of the technique, while tantalizing, remains to be conclusively proven in human trials. However, in June 2006 positive results were announced for a bird flu DNA vaccine and a veterinary DNA vaccine to protect horses from West Nile virus has been approved In August 2007, a preliminary study in DNA vaccination against multiple sclerosis was reported as being effective.

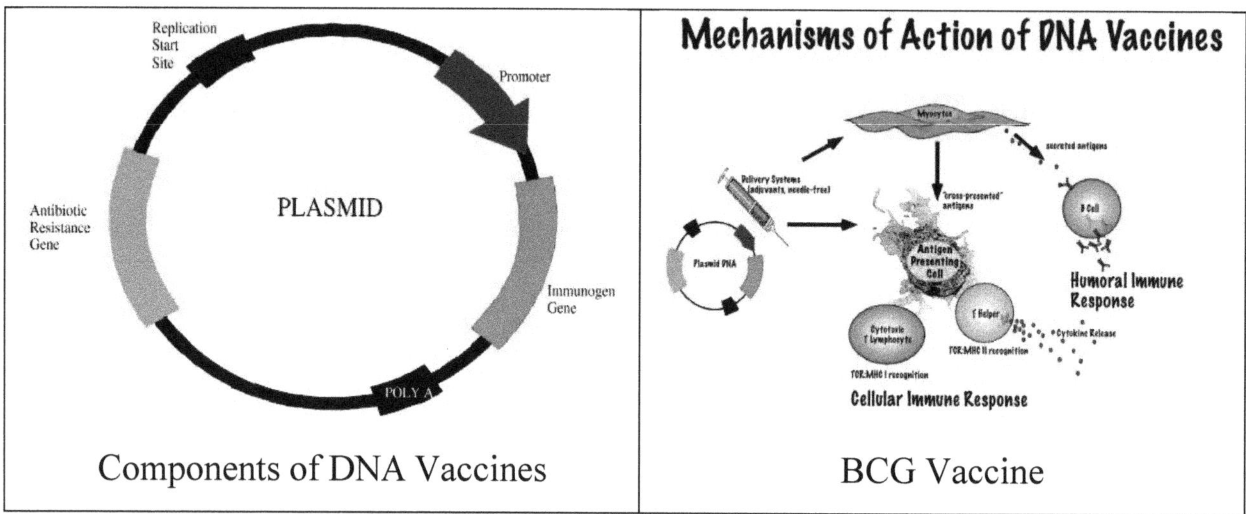

| Components of DNA Vaccines | BCG Vaccine |

06. Advantages and disadvantages of DNA vaccines are listed in the following slide

Advantages	Disadvantages
<ul><li>Subunit vaccination with no risk for infection</li><li>Antigen presentation by both MHC class I and class II molecules</li><li>Able to polarise T-cell help toward type 1 or type 2</li><li>Immune response focused only on antigen of interest</li><li>Ease of development and production</li><li>Stability of vaccine for storage and shipping</li><li>Cost-effectiveness</li><li>Obviates need for peptide synthesis, expression and purification of recombinant proteins and the use of toxic adjuvants ,Long-term persistence of immunogen</li><li>In vivo expression ensures protein more closely resembles normal eukaryotic structure, with accompanying post-translational modifications</li></ul>	<ul><li>Limited to protein immunogens</li><li>Potential for atypical processing of bacterial and parasite proteins</li></ul>

4.4 Monoclonal antibodies and their applications

01. Monoclonal Antibodies are cells derived by cell division from a single ancestral cell. Monoclonals are a class of antibodies with identical offspring of a hybridoma and are very specific for a particular location in the body derived from a single clone and can be grown indefinitely. Monoclonal Antibodies recognize and bind to antigens in order to discriminate between specific epitopes which provides protection against disease organisms.

02. Monoclonal antibodies target various proteins that influence cell activity such as receptors or other proteins present on the surface of normal and cancer cells. The specificity of Monoclonal Antibodies allows its binding to cancerous cells by coupling a cytotoxic agent such as a strong radioactive which then seek outs to destroy the cancer cells while not harming the healthy ones.

03. Tumor cells that are able to replicate endlessly are fused with mammalian cells that produce a specific antibody which result in fusion called hybridoma that continuously produce antibodies. Those antibodies are named monoclonal because they come from only 1 type of cell, which is the hybridoma cell. Antibodies that are produced by conventional methods and derived from preparations containing many kinds of cells are called polyclonal Antibodies.

04. Monoclonal antibodies are artificially produced against a specific antigen in order to bind to their target antigens. Laboratory production of monoclonal antibodies is produced from clones of only 1 cell which means that every monoclonal antibody produced by the cell is the same.

05. Fusion of cell culture myeloma cells with mammalian spleen cells antibodies result in hybrid cells/hybridomas which produces large amounts of monoclonal antibody. The cell fusion resulted in two different types of cells, one with the ability to grow continually, and the other with ability to produce bulk amounts of purified antibody.

4.5 Interferons

01. Introduction:

1. Interferons (IFNs) are a group of signaling proteins made and released by host cells in response to the presence of several pathogens, such as viruses, bacteria, parasites, and tumor cells. In a typical scenario, a virus-infected cell will release interferons causing nearby cells to heighten their anti-viral defenses.

2. IFNs belong to the large class of proteins known as cytokines/molecules used for communication between cells to trigger the protective defenses of the immune system that help eradicate pathogens. Interferons are named for their ability to "interfere" with viral replication by protecting cells from virus infections.

3.   IFNs also have various other functions: they activate immune cells, such as natural killer cells and macrophages; they increase host defenses by up-regulating antigen presentation by virtue of increasing the expression of major histocompatibility complex (MHC) antigens. Certain symptoms of infections, such as fever, muscle pain and "flu-like symptoms" are also caused by the production of IFNs and other cytokines.

02. Members of IFNs:

1.   More than 20 distinct IFN genes and proteins have been identified in animals, including humans. They are typically divided among 3 classes:

1.   Interferon type I:

1.   All type I IFNs bind to a specific cell surface receptor complex known as the IFN-α/β receptor (IFNAR) that consists of IFNAR1 and IFNAR2 chains.

2.   The type I interferons present in humans are:

1.   IFN-α:

    1.   The IFN-α proteins are produced by leukocytes. They are mainly involved in innate immune response against viral infection. The genes responsible for their synthesis come in 13 subtypes that are called IFNA1, IFNA2, IFNA4, IFNA5, IFNA6, IFNA7, IFNA8, IFNA10, IFNA13, IFNA14, IFNA16, IFNA17, IFNA21.

    2.   These genes are found together in a cluster on chromosome 9. IFN-α is also made synthetically as medication in hairy cell leukemia.

2.   IFN-β:

1.   The IFN-β proteins are produced in large quantities by fibroblasts. They have antiviral activity that is involved mainly in innate immune response.

2.   Two types of IFN-β have been described, IFN-β1 (IFNB1) and IFN-β3 (IFNB3) (a gene designated IFN-β2 is actually IL-6). IFN-β1 is used as a treatment for multiple sclerosis as it reduces the relapse rate. IFN-β1 is not an appropriate treatment for patients with progressive, non-relapsing forms of multiple sclerosis.

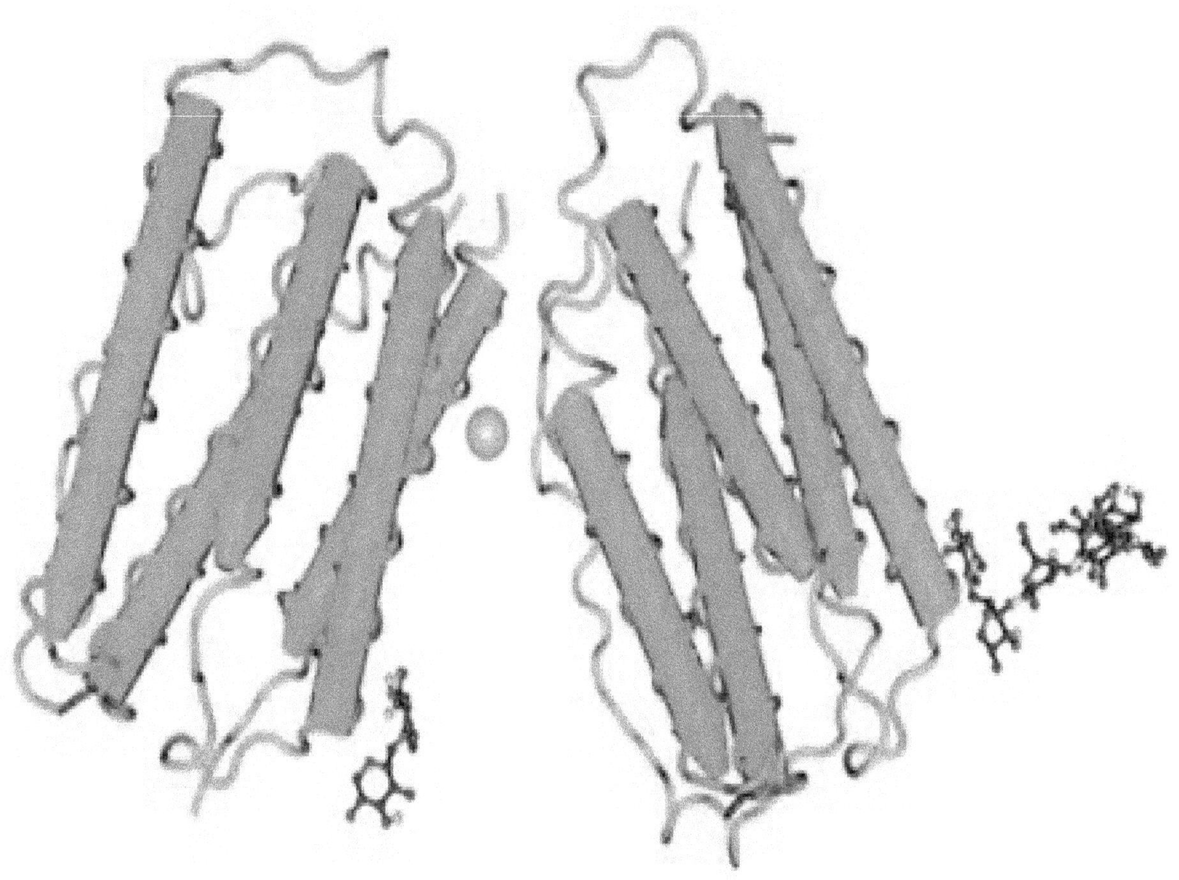

The 3D structure of human interferon beta

2.	Interferon type II:

1.	A sole member makes up the type II interferons (IFNs) that is called IFN-γ (gamma). Mature IFN-γ is an anti-parallel homodimer, which binds to the IFN-γ receptor (IFNGR) complex to elicit a signal within its target cell. IFNGR is made up of two subunits and each of molecules designates IFNGR1 and IFNGR2.

2. IFN-γ is involved in the regulation of the immune and inflammatory responses; in humans, there is only one type of interferon-gamma. It is produced in activated T-cells and natural killer cells. IFN-γ has some anti-viral and anti-tumor effects, but these are generally weak. However, this cytokine potentiates the effects of the type I IFNs.

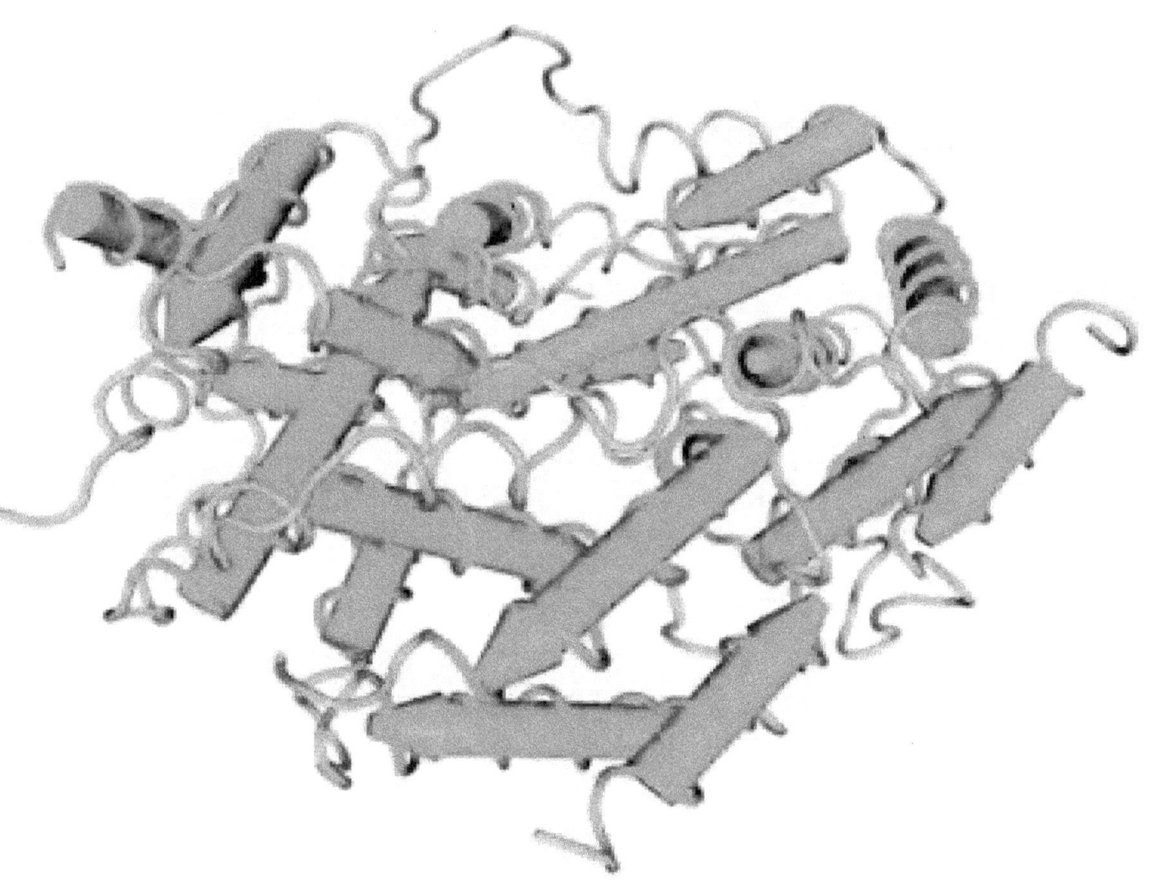

The 3D structure of human interferon gamma

3.   Interferon type III:

1.   The recently classified type III interferon group consists of three IFN-λ (lambda) molecules called IFN-λ1, IFN-λ2 and IFN-λ3 (also called IL29, IL28A and IL28B respectively). These IFNs signals through a receptor complex consist of IL10R2 (also called CRF2-4) and IL28RA (also called IFNLR1, CRF2-12).

2.   Recently, a new protein with a similar function related to IFN-λ3 was found around the same genomic locus and was designated IFN-λ4. Its intracellular signaling was through IFNLR1 and therefore thought to be a type III interferon. However, the evidence of its in vivo bioactivity is still debatable.

03.Cellular functions:

1.   All interferons share several common effects: they are antiviral agents and they modulate functions of the immune system. Administration of Type I IFN has been shown experimentally to inhibit tumor growth in animals, but the beneficial action in human tumors has not been widely documented. A virus-infected cell releases viral particles that can infect nearby cells. However, the infected cell can prepare neighboring cells against a potential infection by the virus by releasing interferons.

2.   In response to interferon, cells produce large amounts of an enzyme known as protein kinase R (PKR). This enzyme phosphorylates a protein known as eIF-2 in response to new viral infections; the phosphorylated eIF-2 forms an inactive complex with another protein, called eIF2B, to reduce protein synthesis within the cell. Another cellular enzyme, RNAse L—also induced by interferon action—destroys RNA within the cells to further reduce protein synthesis of both viral and host genes. Inhibited protein synthesis destroys both the virus and infected host cells.

4.6 Gene therapy

01. Gene therapy (also called human gene transfer) is a medical field which focuses on the utilization of the therapeutic delivery of nucleic acids into a patient's cells as a drug to treat disease. The first attempt at modifying human DNA was performed in 1980 by Martin Cline, but the first successful nuclear gene transfer in humans, approved by the National Institutes of Health, was performed in May 1989. The first therapeutic use of gene transfer as well as the first direct insertion of human DNA into the nuclear genome was performed by French Anderson in a trial starting in September 1990. It is thought to be able to cure many genetic disorders or treat them over time.

02. Between 1989 and December 2018, over 2,900 clinical trials were conducted, with more than half of them in phase I. As of 2017, Spark Therapeutics' Luxturna (RPE65 mutation-induced blindness) and Novartis' Kymriah (Chimeric antigen receptor T cell therapy) are the FDA's first approved gene therapies to enter the market.

03. Since that time, drugs such as Novartis' Zolgensma and Alnylam's Patisiran have also received FDA approval, in addition to other companies' gene therapy drugs. Most of these approaches utilize adeno-associated viruses (AAVs) and lentiviruses for performing gene insertions, in vivo and ex vivo, respectively. ASO / siRNA approaches such as those conducted by Alnylam and Ionis Pharmaceuticals require non-viral delivery systems, and utilize alternative mechanisms for trafficking to liver cells by way of GalNAc transporters.

04. The concept of gene therapy is to fix a genetic problem at its source. If, for instance, in an (usually recessively) inherited disease a mutation in a certain gene results in the production of a dysfunctional protein, gene therapy could be used to deliver a copy of this gene that does not contain the deleterious mutation, and thereby produces a functional protein. This strategy is referred to as gene replacement therapy and is employed to treat inherited retinal diseases.

05.Not all medical procedures that introduce alterations to a patient's genetic makeup can be considered gene therapy. Bone marrow transplantation and organ transplants in general have been found to introduce foreign DNA into patients. Gene therapy is defined by the precision of the procedure and the intention of direct therapeutic effect.

06.Somatic cell gene therapy involves the transfer of gene to a diseased somatic cell either within the body or outside the body with the help of a viral or non viral gene therapy vector.

07.Ex vivo is any procedure accomplished outside. In gene therapy clinical trials cells are modified in a variety of ways to correct the gene. In ex vivo cells are modified outside the patient's body and the corrected version is transplanted back in to the patient. The cells are treated with either a viral or non viral gene therapy vector carrying the corrected copy of the gene.

08.Opposite of ex vivo is what we call in vivo where cells are treated inside the patient's body. The corrected copy of the genes is transferred into the body of the patient. The cells may be treated either with a viral or non viral vector carrying the corrected copy of the gene. If the patient is weak or the cell cannot be extracted out from the body, the gene is introduced directly into the body.

09. Gene therapy done in a restricted area or to a particular site is called in-situ. In situ gene therapy requires the vector to be placed directly into the affected tissues. In vivo gene therapy involves injecting the vector into the blood stream. The vector then must find the target tissue and deliver the therapeutic genes.

10. Methods of Gene Therapy:

1. In situ gene therapy:

    1. In situ gene therapy comprises transfer of corrected copy of the gene into the targeted organ or tissue. The major concern of current time gene therapy protocol is the lack of efficient transduction of the targeted organ. The method is effectively used against cystic fibrosis, a disease of airway epithelium.

    2. The method is also explored for cancer gene therapy where the viral vector is engineered to contain the herpes simplex virus thymidine kinase gene. After injection of the viral vector the patient is treated with a prodrug such as Ganciclovir, which causes 75% reduction in the tumor cell population.

2.   In vivo gene therapy:

1.   Delivery of corrected copy of the gene systemically through injection is a highly efficient way to transfer a transgene to the patient's body. The major problem of in vivo method is its inefficient targeting.

2.   The transgene delivered into the body by means of viral or non viral vector also evokes the immune response. The immune response against the vector leads to its clearance and only transient expression of transgene. The neutralizing antibody does not allow the second injection of the vector. Reducing the neutralizing antibody is the current area of research in order to improve the delivery of gene therapy vector.

3.   All gene therapy delivery protocols require the transgene to cross the plasma membrane and enter inside the nucleus. The major obstacle is still to deliver the transgene effectively to the intracellular compartment.

4.   Many modifications have been suggested into the viral vectors and also non viral vectors to target the gene to the tissue. VP22, a protein of herpes simplex virus has a property to spread from one cell to the other, and this property has been successfully implemented in designing the vectors.

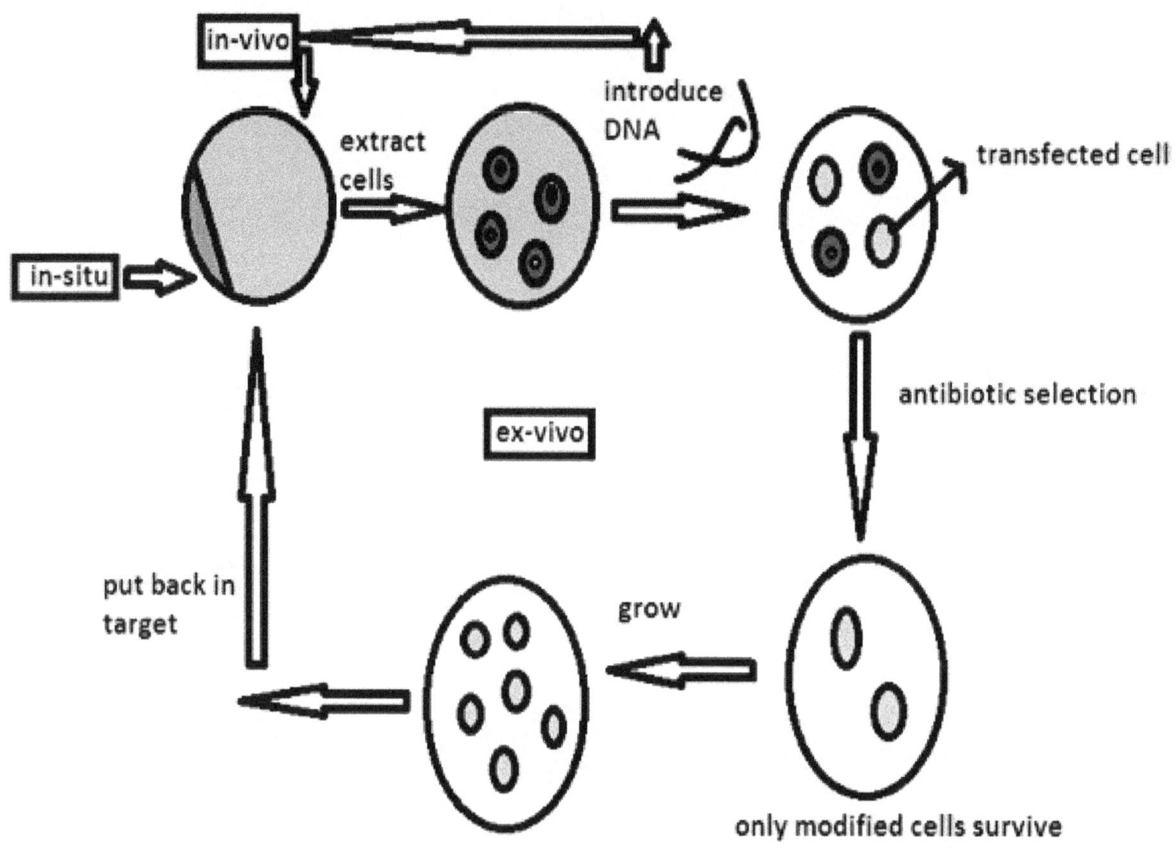

Ex vivo, *in vivo*, and *in situ* gene therapy

Unit 5: Environmental Biotechnology and Bioethics

5.1 Biofertilizers

01. Biofertilizers are defined as preparations containing living cells or latent cells of efficient strains of microorganisms that help crop plants uptake of nutrients by their interactions in the rhizosphere when applied through seed or soil. They accelerate certain microbial processes in the soil which augment the extent of availability of nutrients in a form easily assimilated by plants.

02. Use of biofertilizers is one of the important components of integrated nutrient management, as they are cost effective and renewable source of plant nutrients to supplement the chemical fertilizers for sustainable agriculture. Several microorganisms and their association with crop plants are being exploited in the production of biofertilizers.

03. They can be grouped in different ways based on their nature and function:

1. N_2 fixers:

    1. Free living:

        1. Aerobic – Azotobacter, Beijerinckia, Anabaena
        2. Anaerobic – Clostridium
        3. Faultative anaerobic – Klebsiella

2.   Symbiotic : *Rhizobium, Frankia, Anabaena azollae*

3.   Associative symbiotic : *Azospirillum*

4.   Endophytic : *Gluconacetobacter, Burkholdria*

2.   Phosphorus solubilizers:

1.   Bacteria : *Bacillus megaterium var. phosphaticum, B. subtilis, B. circulans, Pseudomonas striata*

2.   Fungi : *Penicillium sp., Aspergillus awamori*

3.   P mobilizers:

1.   AM fungi

2.   Ectomycorrhizal fungi

3.   Ericoid Mycorrhiza

4.   Orchid mycorrhiza

04. Importance of Biofertilizers:

1. Supplement fertilizer supplies for meeting the nutrient needs of crops.
2. Add $20 - 200$ kg N/ha (by fixation) under optimum conditions and solubilize / mobilize 30-50 kg P_2O_5/ha.
3. They liberate growth promoting substances and vitamins and help to maintain soil fertility.
4. They suppress the incidence of pathogens and control diseases.
5. Increase the crop yield by 10-50%. N_2 fixers reduce depletion of soil nutrients and provide sustainability to the farming system.
6. Cheaper, pollution free and based on renewable energy sources.
7. They improve soil physical properties, tilth and soil health.

Rhizobium	*Azotobacter*
Azospirillum	*Gluconacetobacter diazotrophicus*

5.2 Biodegradation of Xenobiotic compounds

01.Introduction:

1. Xenobiotic compounds are man-made chemicals that are present in the environment at unnaturally high concentrations. The xenobiotic compounds are either not produced naturally, or are produced at much lower concentrations than man. Microorganism have the capability of degrading all naturally occurring compounds; this is known as the principle of microbial infallibility proposed by Alexander in 1965.

2.   Microorganisms are also able to degrade many of the xenobiotic compounds, but they are unable to degrade many others. The compounds that resist biodegradation and thereby persists in the environment are called recalcitrant.

3.   The xenobiotic compounds may be recalcitrant due to one or more of the following reasons:

1.   They are not recognised as substrate by the existing degradative enzymes,

2.   They are highly stable, i.e., chemically and biologically inert due to the presence of substitution groups like halogens, nitro-, sulphonate, amino-, methoxy- and carbamyl groups,

3.   They are insoluble in water, or are adsorbed to external matrices like soil,

4.   They are highly toxic or give rise to toxic products due to microbial activity,

5.   Their large molecular size prevents entry into microbial cells,

6.   Inability of the compounds to induce the synthesis of degrading enzymes, and

7.   Jack of the permease needed for their transport into the microbial cells.

02.Hazards from Xenobiotic Compounds:

1.   The xenobiotics present a number of potential hazards to man and the environment which are briefly listed below:

   1.   Toxicity: Many xenobiotics like halogenated and aromatic hycrocarbons are toxic to bacteria, lower eukaryotes and even humans. At low concentrations they may cause various skin problems and reduce reproductive potential.

   2.   Carcinogenicity: Certain halogenated hydrocarbons have been shown to be carcinogenic.

   3.   Many xenobiotics are recalcitrant and persist in the environment so that there is a build up in their concentration with time.

   4.   Many xenobiotics including DDT and PCB's are recalcitrant and lipophilic; as a consequence they show bioaccumulation or bio-magnification often by a factor of $10^4 - 10^6$.

   5.   They are produced and used in large quantities which favours their accumulation in nature.

2. Bio-magnification occurs mainly because of the following 2 reasons:

1. These compounds are continuously taken up from the environment and accumulated in the lipid deposits of body, e.g., a 100-fold accumulation of DDT by plankton from water,

2. Such organisms are consumed by other organisms in a sequential manner constituting the food chain, e.g., plankton → small fish → large fish → sea-eagles; the concentration of xenobiotics builds up as we move up in the food chain (Table 32.1).

TABLE 31.1. Biomagnification of DDT by continued absorption by plankton and the subsequent passage of planktons and fishes through the food chain (plakton → small fish → large fish → sea-eagle)

Organism environment	DDT concentration	fold increase over concentration in water
Water	0.3 ppb*	--
Plankton	30 ppb	$100 (= 10^2)$
Small fish	0.3 ppm**	$1,000 (= 10^3)$
Large fish	3 ppm	$10,000 (= 10^4)$
Sea-eagle	30 ppm	$100,000 (= 10^5)$

*ppb = parts per billion (1 billion = 1000 million)
**ppm = parts per million (1 million = 1,00,000)

5.3 Legal aspects of genetically manipulated organisms and environment

01.Introduction:

1. Food is one of the most important necessities for humans; we eat to live and at least most people are blesses with a meal a day, while some others can afford three or more. Independent of our culture and customs, dinning remains a vital aspect in different festivities across the world between and within families and friends. Furthermore, we want a healthy and nutritious meal but the question is "How safe is the food we are consuming?"

2. The improvement of plants and livestock for food production and the use of different conservation techniques have been in practice as long as humankind stopped migrating relying on agriculture for survival. With the quest to grow more and better food to meet the demand of our fast growing world population, genetic engineering of crops has become a new platform in addition to plant breeding.

3. Molecular genetics has been and is a very useful tool used to better understanding of genes underlying quantitative traits associated with increasing crop yields or improving food quality. The eagerness to increase crop products has resulted in the genetic manipulation of plants, which has raised much polemics ranging from political, ethical and social problems. Genetically modified food simply means that the original DNA (deoxyribonucleic acid) structure of plants has been altered or tempered with.

4.   Although, there has been steady increase in the total area under genetically modified (GM) crop cultivation, nevertheless, there has been a marked slowdown in the last few years. The most extensively cultivated GM crops include soybean, corn and cotton. Europe is known to grow less than 0.5% of the world's GM crops, primarily because of the very rigorous EU regulations imposed on GMO crops in Europe until 2003 and the refusal of European consumers to buy GM products.

5.   Notwithstanding, the essential knowledge and understanding of cell function and heritability combined with genetic engineering offering new possibilities to transfer and or modify DNA between organisms has enabled governments in many countries, for the first time, to be able to provide adequate food supply to their growing population. These advancements have resulted in the development of efficient vaccines and pharmaceuticals, new food technologies and many other products improving the overall standard of life.

6.   This is also true of agriculture where genetic engineering of crops can complement traditional plant breeding to suit the needs of today's world. Most of these improvements can be grouped under the term "biotechnology", which aims to use organisms, cells and or part of cells in technical or industrial processes.

02.Regulations and why?

1.   Because genetically modified foods have been one of the most controversial topics that have made news in the last years. Many European environmental organizations, NGOs and public interest groups have been actively protesting against GM foods for months. Beside, recent controversial studies about the effects of genetically-modified food have brought the issue of genetic engineering to the forefront of the public consciousness (Fonseca, Planchon, Renaut, Oliveira, & Batista, 2012; Losey, Rayor, & Carter, 1999; Nykiforuk, Shewmaker, Harry, Yurchenko, Zhang, Reed, et al., 2012).

2.   Generally in Europe, the idea of introducing GM food products in the market for human consumption and or as animal feed has not been welcome for health reasons (Maga & Murray, 2010). Although there are no clear research results suggesting the negative effects of GM food to human health, the distancing from GM foods is more or less preventive. Nevertheless, with the growing interest in the use of biofuels as one of the sources of alternative sources energy, genetic engineering then comes in to play for economic reasons.

3.   As a reaction to the growing public concern on GM food and products, many governments across the world have taken different approaches to tackle this hot topic on GM foods. This has resulted in the creation of GMO regulations which are most often country or region specific.

4. The European parliament and council for example have set up regulations regarding GM foods to protect human health and well-being of citizens, and European social and economic interests (McCabe & Butler, 1999). The EU regulations segregates between GM food and feed, it further gives specific instructions on how GM products should be labelled in terms of the amount of modifications involved.

5. EU GMO regulations suggest for example that it is appropriate to provide the combined level of adventitious or technically unavoidable presence of genetically modified materials in a food or feed or in one of its components is higher than the set threshold, such presence should be indicated in accordance with this regulation and that detailed provisions should be adopted for its implementation (Ramon, MacCabe, & Gil, 2004).

6. The possibility of establishing lower thresholds, in particular for foods and feed containing or consisting of GMOs or in order to take into account advances in science and technology, should be provided for.

03.GM food and human health:

1. Food choice is influenced by a large number of factors, including social and cultural factors. One method for trying to understand the impact of these factors is through the study of attitudes. Research is described which utilizes social psychological attitude models of attitude-behaviour relationships, in particular the Theory of Planned Behaviour. This approach has shown good prediction of behaviour, but there are a number of possible extensions to this basic model which might improve its utility. One such extension is the inclusion of measures of moral concern, which have been found to be important both for the choice of genetically-modified foods and also for foods to be eaten by others.

2. It has been found to be difficult to effect dietary change, and there are a number of insights from social psychology which might address this difficulty. One is the phenomenon of optimistic bias, where individuals believe themselves to be at less risk from various hazards than the average person.

3.	This effect has been demonstrated for nutritional risks, and this might lead individuals to take less note of health education messages. Many children in the US and Europe have developed life-threatening allergies to peanuts and other foods. There is a possibility that introducing a gene into a plant may create a new allergen or cause an allergic reaction in susceptible individuals. There is a growing concern that introducing foreign genes into food plants may have an unexpected and negative impact on human health. A recent article published in Lancet examined the effects of GM potatoes on the digestive tract in rats.

4.	Another concern is that individuals do not always have clear-cut attitudes, but rather can be ambivalent about food and about healthy eating. It is important, therefore, to have measures for this ambivalence, and an understanding of how it might impact on behaviour.